STENCILLING

STENCILLING

HELEN BARNETT & SUSY SMITH

Salem House
Topsfield, Massachusetts

First published in the United States by
Salem House Publishers, 1987,
462 Boston Street, Topsfield, MA 01983

The line drawings on
pages 58, 60 and 61 are by Pam Corfield.
All other line drawings by Tessa Land.

Printed and bound in Italy

ISBN: 0 88162 304 0

ACKNOWLEDGMENTS

The publishers would like to thank the following for allowing photographs to be
reproduced in this book:

Adele Bishop USA/Carolyn Warrender Stencil Designs Ltd, London, page 63;
Dragons of Walton Street Ltd, London, page 27; All paints by Dulux, page 47;
Elizabeth Whiting & Associates, pages 23, 35 and 59; Michael Boys
Syndication, pages 11 and 57; Pipe Dreams, page 43; Stencilitis, pages 39 and
55; Stencilitis/Family Circle, page 19.

Also special thanks to Stencilitis, PO Box 30, Rickmansworth, Hertfordshire
WD3 5LG, England, for allowing the reproduction of their original stencil
designs on pages 71–77.

CONTENTS

INTRODUCTION

As a reaction against the mass production of our modern world, many of the oldest and most traditional crafts are experiencing a revival. Patchwork quilts, embroidered samplers, rag rugs and hand-painted pottery exist comfortably in today's interiors alongside the advanced technology and computerized gadgetry we have all come to take for granted. One of the most surprising skills to be covered by this revival is that of decorative paint finishes, and in particular stencilling.

Once they have taken up the cushioned vinyl to strip the floorboards, reinstated fireplaces in blank chimney-breasts and salvaged an antique pine dresser for the kitchen, many people are keen to find authentic methods of decoration for their walls, furniture and fabrics. Stencilling is the most obvious and the simplest method of achieving this rustic, country look. Stencilled images do not have to be synonymous with stripped pine and dried flowers, however. Anything from the elements of nature to aspects of modern urban culture can be used as inspiration for designs, and stencilled patterns can work just as well in a high-tech apartment as they do in a rural cottage.

This book explains how to make the best use of stencils in the home and how they can be used in conjunction with other paint finishes. There is a detailed background to the history of stencilling, discussing its earliest known uses, the countries it originated from and how it began to be used in the home. Colour theory is also covered and it is explained how the various rules can be adapted and applied to decorating interiors.

There is practical advice, too, on making your own stencils and choosing what paints and varnishes to use—from semi-specialist media to the standard domestic ranges available from the local DIY or decorating shop. A chapter on tools and equipment explains the various brushes, knives and other materials that you will need to start stencilling; and a detailed step-by-step guide shows how to use them. Finally, all the areas and surfaces that stencils can be applied to are dealt with—from walls and floors to ceramics, laminates and metal. This includes the preparation of the surfaces, the correct paints, equipment and relevant solvents to use, and how to clean up afterwards.

All this is illustrated with easy-to-follow diagrams, and colour photographs showing stencils used in many different situations around the home.

1 WHY STENCIL?

Stencilling is any method of decorating that involves applying colour through shapes cut out of a sheet of impervious material. It is the art for everyone—a simple method of creating unique and individual patterns, whatever your creative abilities. In our high-tech age of regular edges, smooth polished surfaces and bland colour, a stencilled pattern can excite the eye and lift the spirits.

Stencilling has existed as one of the world's most basic forms of decoration for centuries. But although the methods of application largely remain the same, with each new revival, the sources of inspiration, the choice of colours and the areas of application have changed.

Why has stencilling remained so popular? One of the main reasons has got to be its versatility. Over the years stencils have been made from a varying range of materials, from animal skins to acetate. Usually the colour which is applied to the stencil is paint, but other media can be used. For instance, ground metallic powders such as bronze, aluminium, and even gold and silver can be sprinkled through a stencil on to an adhesive surface to create an exotic and unusual pattern—in fact, the first 'flock' wallpapers were made using wool shavings applied in this way. The most common implements for applying the colour are brushes, but natural sponges, pieces of crumpled fabric, rollers and spray aerosol paint are also often used these days.

So stencilling is not limited to one medium. Nor is it limited to one area of application. Stencilled pattern can be applied to almost any surface, as long as it is more or less flat. To work effectively, the stencil must be kept flat; otherwise the paint will bleed underneath it, which results in smudging and badly-defined edges.

Another point in its favour is that stencilling is extremely cheap to do. The initial outlay for materials such as brushes, stencil card, sponges and paint is soon justified when you find that you're using these basic tools time and time again—especially when the cost of stencilling a wall is compared with what it would cost to wallpaper it. In fact, the cost becomes almost immaterial when you step back to survey the finished work and realize that you have created a unique and original piece of art. For even if you buy ready-made stencils in preference to cutting your own, the end result will never be exactly the same as anyone else's. The colours you choose, the type of paint you use and the article or room where you apply the stencil will all give your work individuality.

The main appeal of stencilling, however, is its simplicity of execution. Whereas hand-painting a design requires less preparation time than stencilling, the application time is much longer, especially when it is to be repeated many times over a large area or on several surfaces. Also, to paint freehand usually requires an accurate outline drawing on the surface to work to. You never need to do this with stencilling. Nor do you need to master a style of brush strokes or indeed be a naturally talented painter or designer.

In short, anyone—with a bit of time, patience and enthusiasm—can create patterns and designs that they might previously have attributed to a professional painter or decorator. The important thing to remember is that there are no rules to conform to other than your own taste and ideas. Inspiration can come from so many sources, whether from elements of nature or man-made forms; stencil designs can feature pastel-coloured flowers intertwined with trellis or black-and-white geometric shapes. The effect can be powerful and dramatic or filigree and subtle. And the joy of stencilling is that it doesn't need to look perfect. In fact, it is often better to achieve a slightly uneven application of colour, or repeated designs that don't quite match up—the charm of stencilling is its handmade quality.

If you don't feel confident about creating your own designs to begin with, it doesn't matter. It's quite acceptable to copy, use ready-cut designs, or start with something very simple. Stencil designs are, by their very nature, stylized, so the images don't have to be an accurate representation of the real thing. Conversely, you can with practice create extremely delicate and complex images, using several colours within one design.

It is difficult to imagine the charm of a stencilled wall or floor if you have never seen one. For inspiration it is well worth a visit to the American Folk Museum near Bath. There you will see the infinite and amazing possibilities of stencilling; suddenly that chair or blanket box you are thinking of stencilling will seem like a much easier project. A visit to this museum makes clear the very real difference between the effect created by a stencilled wall and the more usual alternative of wallpaper. Apart from the obvious difference of a stencil design being a personal one, the stencil artist can tailor his or her ideas to suit any specific interior, by considering its size, shape and particular architectural details, and whether these want to be emphasized or disguised. Windows and doors can be framed with delicate borders; a simple frieze can emphasize, or indeed replace, a picture rail or dado. A chimney-breast can become a focal point with a detailed and more complicated design. Many more individual things can be accomplished with stencils than with wallpaper.

A stencilled design can add definition and improve the proportions of a room. A room with a high ceiling can be visually lowered by the addition of a stencilled border at cornice level and again at dado height or above a deep skirting. Over-large rooms can be given an all-over wall pattern to condense them visually. Continuous borders can lead the eye up a flight of stairs or emphasize a favourite picture or mirror.

Preparation is relatively easy. In the past, most stencilling was applied directly on to plastered walls. It is still feasible to do this, as long as you bear in mind the porous nature of plaster. In most cases, however, it is likely you'll want to apply a base coat of paint first. An easier method is to paper walls with lining paper, which can then be painted—and it is also possible to emulsion over old wallpaper, providing it hasn't begun to lift or blister. Textured paper such as woodchip is more difficult to work on than a flat paper, but it can create some interesting effects. The painted base for stencilling can be flat coats of paint; or, for a slightly more textured look, the lining paper can be sponged, stippled or ragged. It is advisable, certainly for beginners' first projects, to keep the base colours pale and to stencil over in darker tones.

Floors, too, can look really effective when stencilled, and indeed stencilling is the ideal solution if floorboards aren't in good enough condition just to sand and varnish. The design will conceal flaws in the wood, and again, as perfection is not the aim, the occasional bump or knot will all add to the effect. If stencilling a whole floor seems rather a major project, an alternative is to stencil the designs on to hardboard panels. These can be cut to a manageable size, stencilled on a pasting or large kitchen table and, when dry, laid in position. You can varnish the panels either *in situ* or before they are laid.

There is virtually no limit to the many ways in which stencilling can be applied throughout the home. Start with something simple such as a tray or trinket box, and with new-found confidence and enthusiasm you can progress on to bigger things.

2   THE HISTORY OF STENCILLING

Stencilling is usually associated with the early settlers of North America. Primitive wooden furniture, resplendent with images of fruit and flowers, symbolized the preoccupation of those rural communities with the desire for a good harvest. The history of stencilling, however, begins long before this—perhaps as long ago as 3000 BC in China. It is probable that by 2000 BC the Egyptians were using stencils to decorate the coffins of their dead. The precise origins of the process are difficult to pin-point, since early stencils would have been made from perishable materials such as animal skins and vegetation. But the principles of stencilling are so simple that it is very likely to have been used as a method for making patterns by all of the earliest civilizations.

It is known that with the invention of paper by the Chinese around the beginning of the second century AD, paper stencils began to be used as an early form of printing for religious texts and manuscripts. As trade routes opened up between China and its neighbours in both the Orient and the Middle East, a demand was created for stencilled silks, which were worn by the fashionable and wealthy. In Japan and India, too, intricate patterns were stencilled on to fabrics, the inspiration here coming from nature and, especially in India, from geometry. The Japanese perfected the art of creating designs of a particularly fine and delicate nature —it is interesting to note the details which are known about their methods. Thin, rigid sheets were made from mulberry fibre which had been waterproofed with the juice of persimmons. Once the design had been cut, the sheet was covered with an adhesive or varnish, and silk threads or human hairs were used to create a webbing to reinforce the patterns. A duplicate stencil was then glued to the original sheet, and this resulted in a precise and durable template.

Just as trade routes had carried the art of stencilling throughout the East, so their further development took stencils to Europe, most notably to Italy and France. It is generally accepted that the word 'stencil' originates from the old French word *estenceler* (to sparkle) and the Latin *scintilla* (a spark). Beginning in the Middle Ages, the art enjoyed regular and varied use by the French. Playing-cards and games, book illustrations (where stencils were used to colour woodblocked images), textiles and, eventually, wallpaper all featured stencilled patterns.

In England, too, although not quite as prolifically, stencilling was most certainly in use. It appeared initially as wall decoration in the medieval churches of the thirteenth and fourteenth centuries, and by Tudor and Jacobean times was used to create simple geometric patterns on the walls of the larger manor houses. The earliest known example of English wallpaper dates from 1509 and features a stencilled design. Indeed, although other methods using woodblocks were developed for printing wallpaper, stencilling remained a popular method for producing quite complicated designs.

Above, a braid rope stencil pattern breaks the walls into panels inside which a simple fruit and leaf design has been repeated. The overall design has been carefully planned so that the rope braids meet in the corners and frame the doorway.

By the mid-seventeenth century, in a desire to recreate the richness and opulence of the tapestries, brocades and silks which otherwise adorned the walls of domestic interiors, French craftsmen began producing the first 'flock' wallpapers. The pattern was created using a stencil through which a coloured glue was applied, and pieces of shredded remnant wool were sprinkled over it to give a raised, textured pattern. Because of the poor quality of the paper, these wallpapers could not be printed in rolls, but instead were produced in segments called *dominoes*. These dominoes were too inaccurate to be matched to cover large areas, and were also expensive to produce; so they were used individually for feature decoration—over a hearth, in an alcove or, at their most basic, as lining paper for cupboards and drawers. A natural progression from this was for individually stencilled squares to be joined to form lengths of wallpaper and thus hung in adjoining strips over complete walls. In fact a London trade-card from around 1690 indicates that wallpaper was available 'in lengths or in sheets, frosted, or plain'. The cost of production and a general paper tax meant, however, that wallpapers were reserved solely for wealthy customers—more so after 1712, when a duty was introduced on all paper 'printed, painted or stained'.

Thus householders of more modest means were limited to 'direct' stencilling, i.e. applied directly to wood or plasterwork. Many sources from the period refer to its cheapness as a form of decoration. Loudon's *Encyclopaedia of Cottage, Farm and Villa Architecture* of 1836 recommends stencilling because 'This mode of ornamenting walls of rooms is not unsuitable for cottages of the humblest description on account of its cheapness and because in remote places or in new countries, it might be done by the cottager himself, or by the local plasterer or house painter.' Most surviving examples of direct stencilling are therefore to be found in relatively small houses or in the less important rooms of larger ones.

It would appear that the materials used for stencilling have varied enormously through the ages. As a progression from the first method of using animal pelts and leaves for stencils, an extract from Robert Dossies's *Handmaid to the Arts* (1758) recommends the use of thin leather or oilcloth stencils. A later source, *The Modern Painter and Decorator* by A.S Jennings and G.C. Rothery (1920), discusses the advantages and disadvantages of cartridge paper, thick lead foil and 'Willesden paper which, being specially treated in order to make it waterproof, is specially recommended for stencils as it does not require the application of either linseed oil or knotting shellac.'

In the absence of adhesive tapes, the stencils, once cut, were held in place 'by means of specially made pins. These have handles sometimes of wood.' The pigments applied came in the form of oil paint or distemper, to which, it was suggested, beeswax should be added to improve its 'lasting qualities'. Although this information was first published in the 1920s, these methods would have been in use long before then. Its is particularly interesting to note that spraying paint through stencils, which might be considered a relatively recent innovation, is also recommended in *The Modern Painter and Decorator* because 'in addition to the great amount of time saved...a graduation of colour may be obtained...[and] there is practically no risk of colour spreading beneath the surface of the stencil'.

It is clear from documentary sources that stencilled wall decoration was widespread in Britain from about 1790 to 1840. Wallpaper continued as a superior form of decoration, reserved for the wealthy few, as long as it remained expensive. In the mid-nineteenth century, when the tax on paper was removed and it could be produced on the continuous roll by improved machinery, the situation was reversed. Wallpaper ceased to be exclusive, and the craft of stencilling became relatively expensive and therefore fashionable! Having come full circle, stencilled pattern reappeared as wall decoration in churches, chapels and other places of worship. It was also adopted by the artists of the Arts and Crafts movement at the end of the nineteenth century. This was a group of designers and craftsmen, headed by William Morris, who formed a reaction against the mass-production of furniture initiated by the Industrial Revolution. Thus stencilling proved the perfect vehicle for many of their strongly stylized designs, applied to furniture and interiors.

Around the mid-eighteenth century when stencilling was reaching the height of its popularity in Europe, it was adopted as the primary method of decoration by the early settlers on the east coast of North America. Creating and building the rural communities of the New World, these pioneers began to add colour and pattern to their otherwise bleak surroundings. Far away as they were from the fabrics, wallpapers and carpets of home, they strove to imitate these comforts by creating their own designs and methods of decoration. As strips of wood were laid to replace the dirt floors, paint was used to colour them. The earliest designs used simple spatter painting for an arbitrary pattern, but more elaborate designs soon emerged. Stencils made it possible to use repeat patterns as a border around a plain centre, and these eventually became more intricate and complicated. Without the protection of varnish, such floor stencils soon began to fade and wear—thus floor-cloths began to appear as a contemporary alternative to expensive carpeting. Originally these cloths were painted freehand on to canvas, but it soon became evident that stencilling was a faster and more efficient way of producing repeated and intricate designs, and indeed had a unique quality of its own.

As a natural progression, stencilled designs were adapted for use on walls and furniture. Uninhibited by any knowledge of what was currently tasteful or fashionable in Europe, these early American designers produced work of an individual and naïve charm. They drew inspiration from their own surroundings, and emblazoned chests, candle boxes and coverlets with fruit, flowers, leaves, stars and birds. Another recurring image is that of the pineapple, which was a symbol of hospitality. By the early nineteenth century the most popular design was the American eagle, surrounded by stars to represent the number of states in the Union. The colours, too, gave these designs an individual quality. Limited resources necessitated the use of natural dyes; and so the overall impression was one of a rich and mellow nature, in many ways a much more subtle look than that created by the exotic pigments employed in Europe.

Stencilled designs were produced initially by imaginative housewives. Then, as the popularity of the art grew, small bands of professional decorators began to travel the American countryside with a selection of basic brushes, pigments and stencils. In conjunction with the lady of the house, they would devise designs to transform plain interiors into a wealth of pattern and colour by stencilling on to walls, furniture and fabrics. However, as industrialization progressed and the demand for stencilled work exceeded the craftsman's capabilities, commercially produced carpets, fabrics and wallpapers replaced the hand-stencilled work of the earlier generations. Consequently, the hand-produced quality of the stencil was, ironically, adapted for mass production. The early artisans and itinerant stencillers were thus followed by a generation of skilled workmen, who realized the potential of commercially produced stencilled furniture and furnishings. Most famous of these was Lambert Hitchcock, whose name was given to the Connecticut town of Hitchcockville, which grew up around the factory he founded to produce and sell stencilled furniture.

Stencilling remained popular as a method of decoration for many years on both sides of the Atlantic—in fact occasionally in interiors until as recently as the 1940s. However, with the utilitarianism of the war years, plain walls and simple interiors became the vogue, and the craft, by and large, died out. Fortunately, with the recent revival of many traditional crafts and a renewed interest in interior decoration, stencilling is experiencing a new lease of life, and can be seen in many of today's modern homes.

3 COLOUR

Using the right colours when stencilling is just as important as selecting the design. The colours you choose should depend on several factors: the atmosphere and effect you wish to create; the size of the area you intend to cover; and the other elements that are present in the room. This chapter offers a guide to choosing colours for stencilling and how to use them to the best advantage. First, though, it is useful to look at colour from a more general point of view in order to be sure of a good basic understanding of the subject. This is helpful for all aspects of decorating and painting, not just for stencilling.

GAINING CONFIDENCE WITH COLOUR

Colour is all around us. We see it every day in parks and gardens, in the traffic that crowds the streets, on the packets that contain breakfast cereals—indeed, so much so that we take most of it for granted. It will often take a surprisingly clear, blue sky or someone wearing a brightly coloured dress to catch our eye or prompt a comment.

When decorating our homes we are forced to think about colour and how we can use it. Unfortunately most people, lacking confidence, settle for a colour scheme that is unobtrusive and inoffensive and thus, more often than not, very unexciting. This is a shame, because the kind of visual environment we create around us at home can have quite a profound effect on our moods and feelings.

If a room is furnished in drab, unexciting colours, it is unlikely to lift the spirits. Although you might balk at the idea of painting a room yellow, it could have a surprisingly uplifting effect, largely because people relate to yellow as a bright, happy colour.

Unfortunately as adults, we are conditioned to react to colour in an objective and logical fashion, ignoring the way we feel about it. But colour is to do with perception, instinct and emotions, and it is a mistake to become preoccupied with what is right or wrong. Consider the delight of a child when faced with an array of coloured objects, and the uninhibited way in which children will slap paint around, unaware of which colours are 'tasteful' or go together. Trying your hand at stencilling, or any other paint finish, requires an attitude of adventure, of inquisitiveness, and a desire for discovery. It is important not to be bound by convention.

Having said this, there are several widely accepted 'rules' and theories about colour and its application which can provide helpful guidelines for the amateur. For this reason brief sections are included on colour theory and rules that are worth remembering.

COLOUR THEORY

Most people learn about colour systems, such as the colour wheel, at school and then promptly forget it, so some brief revision may be useful.

The seven colours of the rainbow are all pure colours

or hues, undiluted by any other colour. When these colours are lightened or darkened by adding white or black they are referred to as *tints* and *shades*; so pink is a tint of red, and mustard is a shade of yellow. A more commonly used word to describe the level of darkness or lightness of colour is *tone*. Thus the blue tones will be all the different intensities of the colour blue achieved by adding increasing amounts of white or black. Restricting a decorating scheme to the various tones of one colour is one of the safest ways to ensure success. We know the tones will work together, since they are all derivatives of the same colour; but at the same time powder blue and navy, for example, can make a strong statement because of their tonal contrast.

The colour wheel is a visual chart that illustrates the established principles of the structure of colour. Red, blue and yellow are the three primary (or first) colours. Secondary colours are produced by mixing two primaries (orange from yellow plus red, purple from red plus blue, green from blue plus yellow).

If any of the primaries are then mixed with a secondary colour we get tertiaries, and by adding black or white to any of the colours in these three groups we get our tints and shades, or tones. In this way decorators who mix their own paints produce an almost infinite number of colour permutations. You may prefer initially to use ready-mixed colours for your stencilling. However, as you gain confidence you may find that the colours you want for a particular effect or scheme are unavailable as ready-mixed paints, and this is the point at which to begin to experiment.

Use an ordinary paintbox to begin with. By mixing and matching colours on paper, you will understand more about how colours affect each other and get a better idea of how they can be applied to the best advantage.

Another important lesson to be learned from the colour wheel, and subsequently your paintbox, is that of complementary colours. The colours which appear almost opposite on the wheel balance each other visually and are therefore complementary. This knowledge can be a useful guide for balancing a colour scheme. Mixing equal amounts of two complementary colours always produces grey, so adding a little of one colour to its complementary will have a softening effect without altering the basic tone.

COLOUR APPLICATIONS

There are several fairly well known 'rules' about the effect colour can have on a room—how visually it can make a room appear larger, smaller, warmer or colder than it really is. Before applying any of these rules, however, it is important to look carefully at the room and its proportions.

Is the ceiling high or low? Are there any architectural details which you may want to make a feature of, or conversely, disguise? How many doors and windows are there? Are the windows large or small? How much light do they allow in and what kind of light is it—sunny southern or cold northern light? How much will the lighting change at night? (This is a vital aspect of decorating, which you should plan in conjunction with the colour scheme.) What, if any, are the elements of furnishing that may need to be emphasized? For instance, are there wall lights, a picture or a mirror to go on the wall that is being painted? Are there any items of furniture in the room which may influence the colour choice? Last, but not least, what is the style of the room to be? If it is a sitting-room reserved for adults, say, then pale colours are feasible; if it is to have a traditional look, then the colours should reflect that feel. All these factors should influence the way you choose to decorate.

Applying the theory

You will probably know that lighter colours make the

walls of a room visually recede and therefore make it appear larger. In the same way, a ceiling can be visually lowered, or raised, depending on the colour or tone it is painted. The shape of a room and its architectural details can either be given prominence or disguised, again by the colour or tones of the paint. For example, woodwork picked out in a dark colour against lighter walls will accentuate the shapes of windows and doors. The eye will be led around the shape of a room where a picture rail or skirting continues into alcoves or around a bay window. In the same way, a stencilled border, whether at dado, skirting or picture-rail height, will draw attention to the undulations of the wall surface.

If, however, a room is broken up by too many details, the effect can become 'busy' and overpowering. In this case it is wiser to go for unity and to use the same colour, or similar tones of different colours, for both woodwork and walls. The same rules apply if there are aspects of the room you wish to disguise, such as unboxed pipes or a meter box. Painted to match their background, they will be camouflaged; contrasting colours would draw attention to them.

Doors and windows should always be an important consideration when decorating, not least because they provide views to an area beyond, be it a hallway, landing, garden or street. If the view is pleasant, you will want to draw attention to it, in which case a decorative treatment can be employed. This can be done using fabrics or detailed stencilled work or simply by painting their frames in a contrasting colour to the rest of the room. If there is more than one door, you should pay special attention to the views that are seen when you walk into the room. It is from here, after all, that guests will form their first impressions. Apart from the views outside doors and windows, also consider which direction they face and therefore what kind of light they admit—this is another point where colour can be used to compensate. Colours are classified into groups of warm and cold. Blues and greens, particularly when combined with white, will create a cool, fresh atmosphere; this is perfect for rooms flooded with bright summer sunshine, but not so good in the winter when a warm, cosy interior is needed to cheer against a bleak November day. Reds and yellows, on the other hand, can provide the necessary warmth in a north-facing room that gets little or no sunshine.

The reasons for this effect of colour 'temperature' are simple. We automatically associate reds and yellows with warmth because these are the colours of the earth, fire and sun: blues and greens are synonymous with coolness and space because they are the colours of the sea, sky and green fields. When such colours are used in interiors, these associations are made, and so a room will appear to be warm or cold. So these colours can be used to change the atmosphere of a room. When the quality of light is cold, a rich, mellow colour such as terracotta or mustard will give it warmth. A room which gets a lot of natural sunlight can be painted in softer, cooler tones of pale green, blue or white.

These rules can provide useful basic guidelines for choosing colours but, as with all rules, there are exceptions. Depending on the quantity of the various colours used to mix them, there are warm blues and cool reds. So the best way to learn about the effects of different colours on a room—and on each other—is to experiment. Don't recoil in horror as you visualize yourself repainting a room for the third time before getting it right. There are ways to experiment before you actually apply any paint on walls. First, though, you should choose your colours.

CHOOSING COLOURS

The colours you choose for your first and subsequent projects will depend very much on what you intend to stencil. If you are feeling confident you may wish to start by stencilling a border around the walls of a room. But it may be wise to begin with a less ambitious project on a smaller area, where any mistakes are easier to rectify. A piece of furniture such as a chair-back or a chest of drawers is often the best starting-point. The design can be as complex as you wish, but because, for a small area, you won't need many (if any) repeats, it will allow you to get the feel of the process and give a fairly instant result.

The inspiration for choice of colour can come from many sources. Nature is the perfect starting-point, as it provides a wealth of colours that clearly do work together. What could be more stimulating than the golds, browns and reds of autumn leaves, or the vivid contrasts of colours in a summer herbaceous border? In the city, too, inspiration can be found in the colour and contrasts of advertising hoardings, books and magazines. The choice of colour will go hand in hand with the selected design. If a country-cottage feel is what you're after, the traditional stencilling symbols of fruit, flowers, animals and birds will require a range of earthy colours punctuated with bright blues and greens. If a stylized art-deco design such as a sunburst is used, you can combine matt black with gold and cream.

The choice of colour will also depend largely on how realistic you want the design to look. A rose pattern need not necessarily be executed in shades of pink and green; you may want to use the design with a colour scheme of blue and yellow or to achieve the soft greyish look of a design that has faded with age.

For a piece of furniture, the room it is to be kept in and other elements in the room are a fairly good basis for colour choice, and may provide inspiration for the design. For example, in a room where floral fabrics are used you could pick out a part of the fabric design to simplify for the stencil, and thus the colours you use could be matched up to the fabric colours.

On a small area you can get away with a more stark contrast of colours than over a large area. Stencilling generally uses dark tones on a lighter background. Because a stencilled design is usually not solid colour, the background needs to be a contrasting one. This will of course depend largely on the paint and method of application used. A stippling brush will create a more uneven surface of colour than a spray aerosol paint. If you intend to stencil several surfaces in a room, this will need to be carefully planned in advance. The amateur stenciller, with newly acquired confidence, will often end up stencilling everything in sight. This results in drastic overkill, with the eye bombarded by colour and pattern on all fronts. This is not to say that stencilled walls, furniture and fabrics won't work together. In experienced hands, a wide variety of colours and patterns can be combined to create an interior that is exciting and stimulating and has an individual charm. But initially it is probably wise to concentrate on one aspect of a room—either the walls or a couple of items of furniture. Live with them for a while before you add any more stencilling to the room. You may find that these initial designs are enough on their own and that adding other stencilled areas would detract from them.

If a stencilled wall pattern is to be predominant in a room, the colours for the design must show up strongly on a light background. If it is only one of several patterns in a room, then the colours of the stencilled pattern and the background will need to be tonally closer to one another.

Always test selected colours on paper before applying them in position. Paint sheets of paper in the background colour over which the stencil is to be applied. Stencil a couple of repeats of the design, and leave it to dry before making a final judgment—paints change colour, often quite dramatically, when drying. For walls, use sheets of lining paper; when dry, Blu-tack them on to the wall and stand back to get a fairly accurate idea of how the design

Two flower stencil patterns have been used imaginatively as the dominant theme in the furnishings of this room. Combined, they have been used as a border at dado and picture rail height; separately, they cover the walls in place of wallpaper. For a truly co-ordinated style, the tablecloth and knitting basket have been stencilled too.

looks and how the colours work together. You can get away with using much more intense or vibrant colours for a simple stencilled border than if you are repeating a design all over a wall like a patterned wallpaper.

The choice of colours available and how they work together will vary depending on the type of paints used and the method of application. Further details of these aspects are covered in Chapter 4. It is important to remember that juxtaposed colours can change each other. For example, yellow or green will tend to make any blue next to it look lavender. Colours will also appear different in artificial light. It is particularly important to bear this in mind when you are decorating a dining-room or bedroom which will be seen more often at night than in daylight. When testing your colours, always look at them in context with the artificial light that will be used in the room. Varnishing over colours makes them more brilliant and intense but will also yellow them slightly.

4 PAINTS AND VARNISHES

Depending on the surface you intend to cover, there are usually several options for the type of paint you can use. Professional decorative painters use a wide array of media, ranging from traditional finishes such as gesso to special trade eggshells. For the beginner it is wise to stick to a basic range of paints, partly because they are easier to get hold of but mainly because they are simpler to use. Once you have mastered the various techniques of stencilling you may want to diversify, in which case read in greater detail about the more specialist paints and varnishes.

After stencilling for some time you may wish to start mixing your own colours—professional painters and decorators rarely use ready-mixed paints, as their colour ranges are considered too limiting. Although mixing colours is relatively simple, to begin with it is advisable to stick to ready-mixed paints. This does not mean your colours have to be boring. The types of paint suggested in this chapter are generally available in a fairly wide range of colours, and the well-known domestic paint manufacturers all produce mix-to-order ranges.

The main requirement when stencilling is to use a paint which dries quickly. This allows a second or third colour to be added, or top coats of varnish to be applied without waiting days before the design can be finished. The fastest drying paints are water based, as opposed to the other type of paints dealt with which are oil based. As a general rule, use water as a solvent for thinning and

cleaning up water-based paint; and for oil-based paint use white spirit. One exception is included below: spray aerosol paint requires a special solvent—benzol or acetone—for cleaning.

The discussion of paints is divided into two sections. First the best paints for stencilling, which are slightly specialist but available from most good art and craft shops, are dealt with. Then the standard domestic paints are considered, which most readers will be familiar with. Domestic paints tend to be cheaper; they are more easily available, and you may have odd left-over amounts at home which you can use to experiment with.

Whatever type of paint you use, it should be creamy in consistency. Paint that is too watery tends to seep under the stencil and give messy edges.

SEMI-SPECIALIST PAINTS

Artists' acrylics
Acrylic paints are the best all-round stencilling medium. Widely available from craft shops or artists' suppliers, they come in tubes or jars in a wide selection of colours, have a creamy consistency and dry quickly to a matt finish. Acrylics are suitable for use on walls, woods, fabrics that don't require dry-cleaning, unglazed ceramics, some plastics and natural woven fibres such as basketware. They are water soluble and can thus be thinned to create a transparent effect. Alternatively, a

*The doors of this kitchen dresser have been stencilled both inside and out so that the china can be attractively displayed with the doors open.
The fruit basket and apple designs have been applied with spray-on paints to enable a subtle graduation of colour to be achieved.*

special PVA adhesive can be used for thinning; this retains the original consistency, so the solution doesn't become too watery.

The only drawback of artists' acrylics is that they are quite expensive if used to cover a large area, such as an all-over wall pattern. Cheaper alternatives, also suitable for stencilling, are artists' gouache and poster colours.

Japan paint
Japan paint has been a favourite with stencillers for years. Somewhat hard to come by (although, as demand increases, this is changing), it is best obtained through specialist paint suppliers or stencilling shops. Japan paints dry quickly to a matt finish and like acrylics are available in a good range of colours. Being oil based, and thus soluble with white spirit, they are ideal for shiny, non-porous surfaces such as metal, glass, glazed ceramics, shiny plastics and laminates, as well as synthetic fabrics like fake leather. Since these paints are thinner than acrylics, it is important to use a very dry brush; otherwise the design will look messy and may run.

Signwriters' colours
These are very similar to Japan paint, although not available in such a wide range of colours. Because of their thick, opaque nature they give good coverage with one coat and are ideal for floor stencilling. They are available from specialist paint suppliers.

Spray-on aerosol paints
These cellulose paints—normally used for car bodywork—create a very specific effect, a softer, mistier look than the standard method of brush 'pouncing'. They are available in a wide range of colours, including metallics, and they dry almost on contact. However, a bit of practise is needed to master the art of using them. The area surrounding the design must always be masked off, because aerosol paint tends to diffuse over a fairly large area. The stencil must be firmly fixed in place, as the fine spray can filter underneath—don't spray continuously, but use short bursts. Cellulose spray paints can be applied over emulsion or other water-based paints but not on oil-based media. They require a special solvent—benzol or acetone—for cleaning up, and you must make sure you work in a well-ventilated room.

DOMESTIC PAINTS

Undercoat
Undercoat is the flat, slightly chalky paint commonly used on woodwork as a non-porous base coat for oil-based paints. It is relevant to mention it here because some experts use it occasionally for tough, matt, opaque colour. It can be tinted with artists' oil colours or universal stainer (see overleaf).

Emulsion
This term is used to describe a wide range of water-based paints which are readily available from DIY stores and decorating shops. They include the familiar flat emulsion paints and also the newer matt vinyls and satin- or silk-finish emulsions and vinyls. The best of the non-specialist paints for stencilling, emulsions are inexpensive, easy to use and quick drying, and can be applied to a wide range of porous surfaces with brushes, rollers, cloths or sponges. Matt emulsion or vinyl will suit most situations, but a silk or satin finish should be used in damp or steamy areas, such as kitchens and bathrooms. Silk and satin finishes are tougher than matt, have a slight sheen when dry and are washable. (Paint manufacturers claim that matt emulsions and vinyls can be wiped clean, but often stubborn marks won't lift unless a protective varnish has been applied.)

Emulsion paints are generally used on walls. They are ideal for brickwork or bare plaster, as they allow the surface to breathe. But don't use them on metal, because they will corrode it. Emulsions are also suitable for porous surfaces such as wood, unglazed ceramics and basketware. If you intend to stencil emulsion on to an emulsioned base, try the colours on a test area first—emulsion paints remain very porous, even when dry, and can thus soak up colour applied on top.

Because they chip and peel easily, emulsion paints are not recommended for furniture, although a fine varnish will protect them against moderate wear and tear.

Eggshell and mid-sheen paints

There is a specialist trade eggshell (i.e. not available through retail outlets), which is favoured by professional decorators and is superior to other mid-sheen paints. But for the amateur's purposes the readily available eggshell and mid-sheen paints by the well-known domestic paint manufacturers are perfectly adequate.

These oil-based paints give a tough, non-porous finish that looks and feels good and is extremely hard-wearing. When dry, the surface has a soft, light sheen much less shiny than that of gloss paint. It is thus ideal for woodwork and walls, although being oil based each coat will take twelve to sixteen hours to dry. Although these paints can be used for stencilling, they are not ideal because of their drying time—they are, however, good for creating solid or distressed background finishes on furniture, walls and small wooden items such as trays which need a tough, chip-resistant surface (see Chapter 7).

Gloss paints

These days you can choose from semi-gloss, gloss and brilliant gloss finishes to achieve the required effect. Gloss paints provide a long-lasting finish that is moisture resistant, easy to wipe clean and virtually chip- and scratch-proof. Most commonly used for furniture, window frames and other woodwork, gloss can be used on walls, although it creates an effect somewhat reminiscent of old-fashioned schools and hospitals. If you intend to stencil over gloss paint, it is necessary to sand the top coat lightly, in order to provide a key for your design to adhere to. Gloss paints must be used over a proprietary undercoat and need between twelve and sixteen hours to dry.

OTHER MEDIA

Universal stainers

Universal stainers are highly concentrated colours which are added to paint to change its colour. You will need these tinting agents in order to mix your own colours. This can also be done using acrylic paints or other forms of pigment, but universal stainers can be obtained from most paint suppliers and, although oil based, they can be mixed with almost any type of paint.

Stains

Wood stains are alternatives worth considering when you are treating furniture, floors or any other wood that is in fairly good condition. Instead of the opaque finish provided by paint, stains tint the wood with transparent colour, allowing the wood-grain to show through. Some stains just colour the wood and will need one or more coats of protective varnish, depending on the area you are treating. Others incorporate a hard-drying oil varnish which dries to a tough, shiny finish. This type usually require a light sanding before paint can be stencilled on top.

Metallic powders

Sometimes known as 'poor man's gold', metallic powders are available in several finishes ranging from silver to three shades of gold. The powders need a binding agent (most manufacturers can supply one) to give them the correct consistency for stencilling. Standard stencilling brushes and 'pouncing' methods are used to apply them.

Varnishes

The various traditional types of varnish have been largely superseded by polyurethane varnish, which is cheaper, more versatile and easier to use. Suitable for walls, woodwork, floors and furniture, polyurethane varnish is available in matt, semi-gloss and gloss finishes and doesn't have a tendency to yellow like the old-fashioned varnishes do. Gloss varnish, like gloss paint, dries to a very tough and shiny finish. It can, however, make your designs look rather cheap and gaudy; where possible, it is preferable to use the matt or semi-gloss finish. Matt varnish dries with no shine and thus protects without changing the effect of the painted surface; semi-gloss is slightly tougher and dries with a soft sheen that looks good over most decorative techniques. Although touch dry in six to eight hours, polyurethane varnish should be left overnight before another coat is applied.

Caution: spray-on aerosol paints should be sealed with a spray varnish, as brushed-on varnish can smudge the design.

Shellac

Shellac is an old-fashioned wood varnish still sometimes used by professional decorators. It is not recommended as a strong finishing varnish, as it is not water- (or alcohol-) proof. However, it may come in useful as a barrier coat to isolate any area of stencilling which shows a tendency to bleed, and to build up a smooth surface for further decoration.

5 TOOLS AND EQUIPMENT

Making your own stencils is easy once you have mastered a few simple techniques, and it requires little initial outlay on tools and materials. Add to the basics when you need to and as you become hooked! The following is a comprehensive guide to the equipment needed for stencilling, from cutting your own designs to painting and applying protective layers of varnish.

STENCIL MATERIALS
The main requirements for a stencil are that it must be both resilient and impervious.

If you are making a stencil intended only for limited use—when stencilling a chair, for instance, or a small box—then it is possible to use stencil paper. Inexpensive and readily available from art and craft suppliers, this is a semi-transparent waxed paper that allows a stencil to be cut from a design placed directly underneath.

More robust is the traditional dark yellow coloured stencil card. This thick flexible board has been pre-soaked in linseed oil, which gives it a smooth, impervious surface that is easy to cut. Unlike the thinner stencil paper, it is not transparent, so designs must be transfer-red on to it before cutting.

The best stencils are made from clear acetate, a relatively new and quite expensive material. Available in a variety of thicknesses, it is extremely durable, and if treated carefully will last for years. Because it is transparent, designs can be traced directly on to it using a

technical, marking pen, doing away with the need for carbon paper. This is particularly helpful if you are working on a design using a variety of colours and need to cut two or three individual stencils for each colour. If you are not used to cutting stencils, choose simple geometric designs to begin with, since acetate tends to cut or split when intricate curved shapes are cut into it. The great advantage with acetate stencils is that any build-up of paint can be easily spotted and quickly cleaned off.

1 *A technical marking pen is used for transferring designs directly on to clear acetate. The advantage of using acetate is the speed with which a stencil pattern can be produced. Simply place the acetate sheet over your chosen design; trace out the outline with the marking pen; and then carefully cut out.*

The surfaces in this kitchen have been extensively stencilled using large rose bouquet stencil designs. The effect is prevented from becoming overbearing, however, as soft shades of pink and green have been used.

CUTTING BOARDS

You can cut stencils on a variety of surfaces. Glass is preferable to wood because score marks or dents on a wooden board can jolt the blade and cause the acetate to tear. Cover all the edges of the glass with masking tape for safety. If you prefer not to use glass it is possible to buy self-healing cutting boards made from special plastic. They close up cut lines once you lift the knife blade, and leave no ridges. They usually have a grid printed on top which helps when trying to cut accurate straight lines.

A sheet of plywood, chipboard or blockwood is perfectly adequate for cutting stencil card or paper. If you don't have any of these to hand, a vinyl tile or piece of linoleum will do.

KNIVES

A craft knife with replaceable blades is ideal for both stencil card and acetate. Make sure that you always use a sharp blade to ensure precise, clean edges.

When you become more proficient and want to start cutting more intricate designs, a scalpel blade may be useful. Tap out neat, round circles using a hammer and hole-puncher, but remember to do this only when the stencil is resting on a piece of wood—glass will shatter.

APPLICATORS

Whether you are a beginner or an experienced stenciller it pays to invest in the best brushes you can afford; not only will they do the job more efficiently, but they last longer, too. A top-quality brush should have a thick, flexible filling, firmly secured in a comfortable and well-balanced handle.

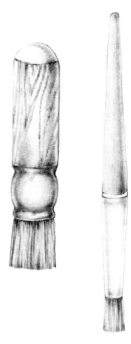

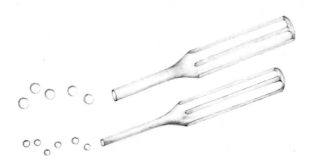

2 *Hole-punchers come in many sizes and can be used, in conjunction with a hammer, to tap out neat circles from stencil card and acetate.*

3 **Left** *The traditional stencilling brush is short and stubby. The stiff hogshair and blunt end is ideally suited to the 'pouncing' motion required when stencilling.* **Right** *The fitch brush is smaller making it suitable for detailed work and for retouching designs.*

The traditional stencil brush is short and fat, looking rather like a man's shaving-brush. It comes in various sizes from 6 mm to 50 mm (⅕ in to 2 in)—choose according to the size of the stencil opening; the larger the opening, the larger the brush should be. These thick brushes are usually made from hogshair and are cut bluntly across at the end, which makes them the ideal shape for the typical 'pouncing' or vertical dabbing motion used when stencilling. In this way the paint is stippled through the stencil holes, allowing you to control the depth of colour and to achieve subtleties of shading, thus giving a slightly rustic, handmade quality. Lightly 'pouncing' colour on like this also means that there is less likelihood of paint seeping under the stencil.

For intricate detailed work and retouching designs you may find a smaller fitch brush more suitable.

If you want to have a go at stencilling with equipment you may have at home, before investing in specialist brushes, you could adapt an ordinary domestic brush by cutting the bristles down to around 2.5 cm (1 in). Remember to use the brush with only a light pressure; if you press too hard the bristles will splay out and give your work an untidy edge.

All the brushes mentioned so far give finished stencils a stippled or orange-peel texture. With some patterns it is possible to introduce a different texture by using various other paint applicators. Sponges create a random splashed effect, and by varying the grade of sponge from coarse natural sea sponges to fine synthetic cosmetic sponges you can achieve a whole range of different effects.

Small pieces of fabric will create a soft, watermarked effect, which again can be varied according to the fabric type you choose. Soft velvets and velours produce particularly interesting results. Paint-pads and rollers are another alternative if the cut-outs of the stencil are not too detailed.

Whatever applicator you choose, remember that the secret to crisp, professional-looking designs is not to overload it with paint.

EXTRA ITEMS

For transferring designs on to the stencil card you will also need a fine fibre-tipped pen, a small-gauge knitting-needle, a supply of tracing paper and carbon paper. Keep a ruler handy for accurate positioning of the stencil, and masking tape to hold it securely in position when painting. Use masking tape in preference to other sticky tapes—it peels off without damaging the surface.

White chalk or a soft pencil is useful for marking the position of a design on floors, walls or furniture, and a plumb-line helps ensure that patterns on walls are straight.

When it comes to painting, use a separate saucer for each paint colour. Have a bottle of solvent appropriate to the paint, and a supply of clean rags on hand.

CLEANING UP

It is important to look after stencilling equipment properly if it is going to last. When you buy a new brush, twirl its head between the palms of your hands to remove any loose hairs, give it a good wash in white spirit and then twirl it dry.

Make sure, when working, that you use a different brush for each colour group, and if you need to clean clogged or caked bristles wipe them with a rag dipped in the appropriate solvent. You should always clean brushes well after each use; with oil-based paint use white spirit, then wash in lukewarm soapy water and rinse thoroughly; with water-based paints like emulsions, acrylics and fabric paints, rinse first in cold water, then wash in warm soapy water and rinse again. Always hang brushes up to dry—if they rest on their tips the bristles will become distorted and weakened. Secure them with a rubber band to ensure they keep their shape, and once dry store them flat.

If you are in the middle of a project and just want to leave paintbrushes overnight, those used with oil-based paints can be left suspended in a mixture containing equal parts of white spirit and raw linseed oil. Before use, rinse them in solvent and twirl dry. Keep brushes used with water-based paints in a polythene bag.

How you clean a stencil will to a certain extent depend on the type of paint you have used in the first place. With a spray paint or water-based paints, wipe the excess away from the stencil holes after use to prevent the size of the design diminishing, then leave out to allow any build-up of paint to dry completely.

If you are working with oil-based paints, however, it is important to wipe the stencil down as you paint, and when you finish to wipe it carefully on both sides with a cloth dipped in white spirit.

Clean off any adhesive from the masking tape using either white spirit or lighter fuel. If you accidentally tear or break any part of a paper or card stencil, apply clear, strong, matt-finish tape to both sides of the tear and trim the excess away with a craft knife.

WORK AREA

A mention should be made here of the area you choose to work in. Whilst it is not essential to have a room set aside for designing, cutting and painting stencils, it does help if you clear an area large enough to house all the tools and equipment whilst you are working.

6 DESIGNING AND CUTTING STENCILS

CREATING A DESIGN

For the beginner there are a wide variety of pre-cut and ready-to-cut stencil designs available. These allow you to master the basic techniques involved in the craft and to gain confidence in your skills. As you become more proficient, however, you will want to try your hand at the exciting and rewarding task of creating your own original designs.

The source of inspiration for stencils is, as has already been said, limitless. Everday objects like flowers and plants in the garden, a bowl of fruit or the family pet can yield a suitable design. More ambitious stencillers may prefer to take their inspiration from works of art, architecture, porcelain or furniture. Others may use their skills to personalize a room, picking out a motif or pattern from an existing carpet, wall covering or fabric and using it to form a co-ordinated border along the floors and walls or around a window.

During the first few attempts at design it is best to stick to simple outlines—the easiest stencils are made from a single symmetrical motif (fig. 4). To make a stencil like this, first pick an interesting silhouette with matching sides; geometrical forms like squares and triangles, leaves or flower-heads are all ideal. Draw half the design along the fold of a piece of paper and cut it out to produce the basic stencil. You can then transfer this to hard-wearing oiled board or clear acetate. More complex and delicate cut-outs can be achieved in this way by folding the paper

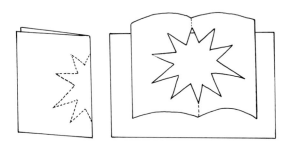

4 *A symmetrical design is the best choice for novice stencillers. Draw half the design along the fold of a piece of paper (left) and cut out to complete (right).*

once or even twice more (fig. 5, page 32).

When you come to attempt the design of an asymmetrical stencil, remember that to begin with it is advisable to choose strong, interesting shapes that are easily recognizable. If you are familiar with ready-made stencils you will have noticed how the objects that they copy have been simplified as they are reproduced. Three-dimensional forms become two dimensional, and the outlines of an object are exaggerated so that they form interesting geometric shapes and patterns. It is this technique that you should aim to copy, creating a series of shapes that can be easily cut out as a flat pattern and which will not create a visually confusing end result.

The beauty of stencilling is that simple designs are just

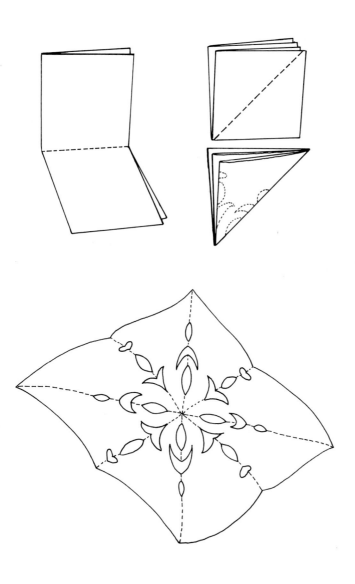

5 *A more intricate pattern can be made by folding the paper two, or even three times.* **a** *Fold a piece of paper in half and then in half again.* **b** *Now fold along a diagonal line, draw a pattern along two sides as shown and cut out.* **c** *Open out the completed stencil.*

as attractive as more complex ones, so anyone—whatever their level of artistic skill—can have a go. If you don't feel confident enough to sketch real-life objects, try using a photograph as a reference instead; its two-dimensional flat image will be much easier to copy. Alternatively trace your design from a picture in a book or magazine, or a flat object like a leaf.

SINGLE STENCILS

A single stencil has the whole design on it and is usually printed in only one colour. To help show detail within this type of design it is therefore necessary to use bridges or links. These thin connecting strips literally bridge the cut-out shapes and extend on to the bordering edges to give strength to the design and hold it together. Try to make these links form a creative part of the design, working with, and not against, it. Bridges cut across a long, flowing line, for instance, make an interesting pattern and also help to prevent the stencil outline becoming distorted when it is painted. To be most effective they should occur at regular intervals; but try to avoid too many intersecting lines, or they will break up the design and make it difficult to decipher when reproduced.

Using the contours and natural shading of the object as a guide, draw lines to follow the shapes they make, and then broaden these lines to form the bridges (figs. 6 and 7). The width and number of links will of course vary according to the size and intricacy of the stencil; large, heavy designs need only a few wide bridges, whereas small, complex patterns will require many narrow linking strips to balance the greater number of cut-out areas. Take care with stencils like this, however, that you do not make the link strips narrower than 1.5 mm ($\frac{1}{16}$ in); if you do they will be too fragile to withstand normal usage.

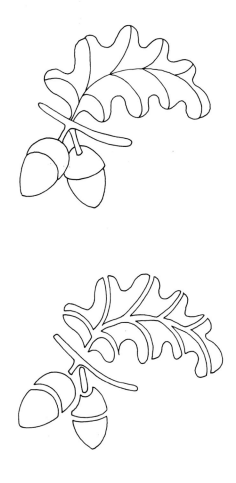

6 *The fragile, long-stemmed shape of a daffodil (left) can be used for a stencil pattern with the help of bridges (right). The bridges form a creative part of the design adding interest to the pattern while also preventing the stencil outline from becoming distorted when it is painted.*

7 *The natural curves of the acorn and the veins on the oak leaves (top) make perfect bridges which work with the shape of the pattern rather than against it*

TRANSFERRING DESIGNS TO THE STENCIL BOARD

Once the design is finalized, you can transfer it on to your chosen stencil board, ready to cut out.

Work out how much board you need for the design, remembering to allow a margin of at least 2.5 cm to 6.5 cm (1 in to 2½ in) around the edge to give strength and rigidity. If you intend to stencil using a paint roller, leave a wider margin of around 7.5 cm (3 in). Clear an area to work on and lay your cutting surface down. If you have decided on stencil paper or board the easiest way to transfer the design is to sandwich carbon paper (carbon side down) between it and the board, securing it firmly with masking tape. Using either a very hard pencil or the tip of a fine-gauge knitting-needle, trace around the lines of the picture. You can then go round the design to clarify it using a fine, dark, fibre-tipped pen or a sharp pencil.

If you prefer not to use carbon paper, trace your design on to a piece of tracing paper, using a soft pencil. Go over the motif again on the reverse side of the paper, leaving as thick a layer of graphite as possible. Place the tracing (reverse side down) on to the stencil board, secure it with masking tape and go over the design again with a harder pencil, using a heavy pressure to transfer its outline. You can then remove the tracing paper and sharpen up the image.

Using acetate is easiest of all. Simply lay the sheet directly over the design and transfer the motif using either a sharpened chinagraph pencil or technical drawing pen.

CUTTING OUT

Now comes the exciting or nerve-racking part! Whether you are using acetate or oiled board, first make sure that you fix it securely to the cutting surface with masking tape to prevent it sliding around. If you are using glass as the cutting surface, it is a good idea to cover the edges with tape to protect you hands.

Pick up the craft knife and, holding it firmly, almost as you would a pencil, begin to cut directly on the inked-in lines of your motif (fig. 9). Try to maintain an even pressure on the knife blade—this will help you keep up a smooth, continuous cutting action. It may help to steady your hand if you rest your little finger on the board. Cut slowly, manoeuvring the board as you work so that the blade of the knife is always coming towards you. This

8 *When transferring a stencil design to stencil board it is important to allow a good margin of stencil board around the pattern to give rigidity. Sandwich a piece of carbon paper with the carbon side down between the stencil board and your design. Secure firmly with masking tape. Trace around the lines of your design using a hard pencil.*

A deep stencilled border runs around the top of this Art Deco style room. The main stencil pattern takes its shape from the distinctive, curved, glass-fronted cabinet in the corner of the room, and a delicate, green, cloud stencil pattern is interwoven to soften the effect.

allows you to keep up a fluent movement which is essential when it comes to cutting round circular and curved shapes. Replace the knife blades frequently to ensure they never blunt.

It is best to start in the middle of a design so that you don't put too much strain on the stencil board when larger areas have been cut away. For the same reason, try to deal with smaller shapes before you move on to the larger ones; nail-punches are ideal for small holes, but never use them on glass. If you are using stencil board, you can try bevelling the edge as you cut. This helps to prevent paint creeping under the rim when colour is applied. To do this, hold the blade at a slight angle of around about 45°–it's not easy but is worth a try. If you

have cut past any of the drawn outlines by mistake, just seal them up again on both sides with a clear, strong adhesive tape, making sure you trim away any excess. Finally smooth any rough jagged edges with fine sandpaper.

MULTIPLE STENCILS

As you gain confidence you can progress to more complex and multi-colour designs which require a separate stencil for each colour. These multiple stencils also allow you to eliminate bridges (fig. 11) and to divide particularly intricate patterns into sturdier sections less likely to tear or break (fig. 10).

To print more than one stencil on top of another presents a new problem: registration, or lining up each stencil accurately to prevent overlapping and messy end results. With clear acetate there is no problem: you draw in a few key lines from another stencil and align them when you begin painting. With opaque stencil board it is slightly more difficult. Trace and cut each component part of the final design, then align all the stencils together so that they form the motif perfectly. Trim the boards so that they are exactly the same size and then either cut notches through the sides of all the boards at once, or

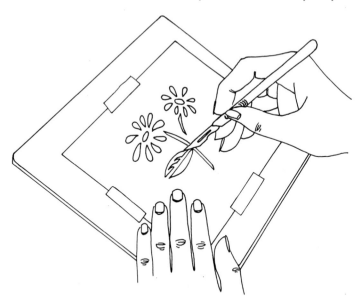

9 *Use a craft knife to cut out the stencil. Holding the knife almost like a pencil and manoeuvring the board so that the knife is always coming towards you will help maintain a smooth, continuous action.*

10 *Intricate designs like this handle can be divided into sturdier sections, which are less likely to tear or break, by using more than one stencil pattern.*

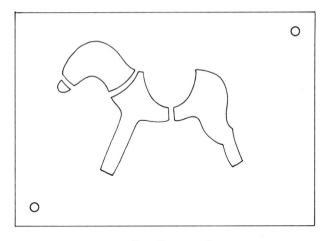

a *Stencil pattern 1*

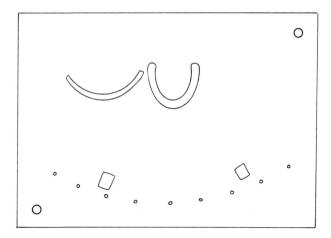

b *Stencil pattern 2*

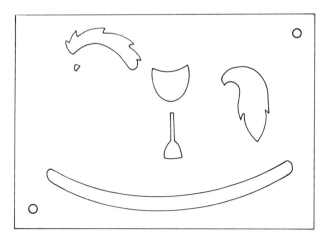

c *Stencil pattern 3*

d *Finished stencil*

11 *The use of a number of different stencil patterns for this rocking horse design not only eliminates the use of bridges but also allows the use of more than one colour. Small holes are punched in the top right and bottom left of each stencil pattern to enable the user to line up each one accurately.*

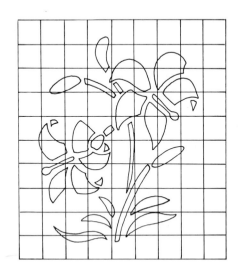

12 *To enlarge a stencil first draw an accurately spaced grid over your original design
(left). To double the size of the design draw out a grid with squares double the size and
copy the design square by square until complete (right).*

punch holes out with a hole-punch. Use these holes to make small pencil registration marks on the surface you are decorating and match up each stencil in turn.

CHANGING THE SIZE OF THE DESIGN

The easiest way to enlarge or reduce the size of the original stencil drawing is to use a photocopying machine which provides this facility. Most local libraries have one for public use. If you don't have access to a photocopier,

however, you can use a measured-out grid to change the size of designs. To do this, first draw an accurately scaled grid over your original drawing, using for instance 2.5 cm (1 in) squares. To double the size of the design, draw up another grid with 5 cm (2 in) squares and carefully copy your motif on to it one square at a time. (See fig. 12.) To reduce a picture to half its original size, do the same thing with a grid of 1.25 cm (½ in) squares, and so on.

A stencil border runs along the top of a room to draw attention to the unusual sloping ceilings. The rose design in peach and green echoes the curtain fabric design.

REPAIRING STENCILS

If a stencil becomes torn (this usually happens on bridges) stick masking or a clear, strong, adhesive tape on both sides of the stencil and carefully trim off any excess. If a section of the stencil has been torn right off, you will need to replace it. Using either the piece of broken stencil itself or the original drawing, trace the torn shape on to the stencil card. Cut out the replacement and tape it in place on the stencil, again trimming off excess tape (fig. 13).

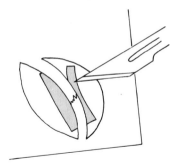

13 *Repairing a stencil*

7   STENCILLING TECHNIQUES

PREPARATION

Before beginning to stencil your chosen design you must first ensure that the surface to be stencilled has been adequately prepared if the results are to be successful and lasting. It is foolish to spend hours painting an intricate stencil, only to discover when it is finished that all you have managed to do is successfully highlight the uneven and cracked surface underneath!

Spend time sanding down woodwork and plaster: fill in any cracks or holes; and make sure that new surfaces are thoroughly sealed. Now the background can be painted with your chosen colour.

Background finishes and colours

Light backgrounds are the easiest to stencil onto—what you are doing is clearly visible, and the stencil colours will retain the same tones. Medium- or dark-coloured backgrounds often show through the stencil paints and can considerably change their appearance; don't dismiss them, though, as they can be used to create very original and dramatic stencilled effects.

Remember, too, that it is not just colour that can add individuality. By varying the method of paint application you can produce a whole variety of textural qualities to the background. Dabbing with natural sponges gives a mottled broken colour; rolling on to the surface with pieces of rag produces the look of crushed fabric; and brushes used for stippling or colour-washing can give the background a distressed or antiqued appearance when used a certain way.

Depending on what you are stencilling there are various types of paint to use for the background (see Chapter 4). Easiest and cheapest to apply are water-based paints like emulsion. Tougher and more durable are oil-based eggshell, gloss and special glazes. Use your test stencils to experiment with colour, texture and so on.

More detailed information on preparation techniques is given in Chapter 8.

EQUIPMENT

The next step is to gather together all your basic equipment. Ensure that you have a pencil and ruler for marking out the surface, masking tape for attaching stencils, palette knives, spoons and a selection of small plates or saucers for mixing paint colours. Also collect plenty of clean rags and the relevant solvent for the paint you are using, stencil brushes (if you are using a multi-colour stencil allow one brush per colour), and of course your stencil.

Make plenty of space to work in: whether it is a small box or a complete floor you are stencilling, it is best not to be cramped. If you can, choose a work area with plenty of natural light, where you will be able to sit or stand comfortably. When stencilling walls and floors, however, you will just have to make the most of the conditions as they are.

MIXING THE PAINT

With practice anybody can achieve perfect results, but no amount of skill or talent will help unless the paint you are working with is mixed to the correct consistency. Fig. 14 shows what happens when the paint is too dry or too wet.

Very little paint is taken on to the brush when it is dipped into the saucer each time, as it has a tendency to dry quickly—so don't be tempted to mix up vast quantities. Start with about a saucerful—you can always mix more as and when you need it.

So many paints can be used for stencilling that it is difficult to give specific guidelines for mixing each one to the correct consistency. The best thing to do is to test the paint out, using your stencil and scrap paper, until you achieve the perfect print. Try the paint first undiluted, as some household emulsions may be the right thickness. If the resulting print is too dry then you can gradually blend in small amounts of the appropriate solvent until you achieve a satisfactory result. Remember to make a careful note of the amount of solvent added—you may need to mix further quantities of paint at a later stage.

Keep a constant check on the paint as you work, correcting its consistency whenever it begins to dry out.

TEST STENCILS

The importance of a test stencil has already been mentioned briefly. It enables you to try out the colour and consistency of your paint. It also allows you to check whether any last-minute alterations to the design are necessary and, most important of all, to familiarize yourself with the basic brush techniques involved. It is always better to make mistakes on a piece of scrap paper than on the wall or furniture you have carefully prepared.

ATTACHING THE STENCIL

Before applying colour, secure the stencil to the surface to

a

b

c

14a *The paint was mixed too thin on this stencil with the result that the effect is rather faint*
b *Here the paint is too thick, which allows it to creep under the stencil pattern and distort the outline*
c *The paint was mixed to the right consistency for this stencil and a perfect effect is the result*

be decorated. This will prevent it slipping around as you work, and will help stop paint from running under the edges and smudging the design.

Use small pieces of masking tape to attach the stencil (ordinary clear tape will pull the surface off when you remove it). It is a good idea to test the tape first on an

Two intricate rose patterns have been stencilled around an elegant claw-and-ball-foot bath. On the wall, these designs have been adapted and combined together with a vase design to create a focal point in the room.

unobtrusive area to double-check that it will not damage the surface.

When using aerosol paints, protect the area around the stencil from drifting paint spray. Use lining paper or newsprint secured with masking tape.

BASIC STENCILLING TECHNIQUES

The stencil is in position, the equipment neatly set out close to hand. You are now ready to begin applying colour.

Using brushes

Pick up the stencil brush and dip the tips of its bristles into the saucer of pre-mixed paint. Using a vigorous action, jab the bristles on to a clean piece of scrap paper. This helps remove any excess paint and also distributes the paint evenly through the bristles. Continue jabbing the bristles until the marks they leave on the paper have a soft, shaded quality.

Hold the stencil brush like a pencil, with your fingers close to the bristles. Keeping the tips of the bristles flat to the surface, begin to dab up and down with the characteristic pouncing action through the cut areas in the stencil. Your test samples will teach you how much pressure to apply to discharge paint quickly and effectively from the brush on to the surface. With this stencilling technique the wrist should remain flexible and relaxed. The fingers of the other hand should be used to hold the stencil flat, to guard against the bristles of the brush slipping under the edges or snagging on intricately cut areas.

It is generally best to work in from the edges of a design, establishing the shape of the stencil first and then working towards the middle. The aim is to build up colour gradually: so, instead of concentrating on one area, work the stencil brush in circular movements, clockwise and anti-clockwise, until the shapes are filled.

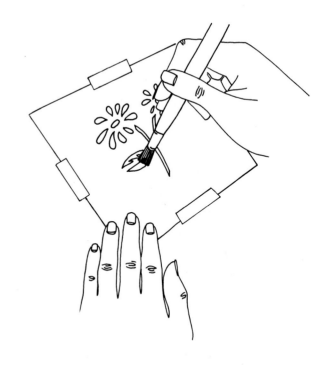

15 *Applying paint to make a stencil using the 'pouncing' action. Once you have the correct amount of paint on the brush, dab up and down on the cut areas of the stencil, working from the edges inwards.*

Remember as you build up the colour of the motif, that even dark shades appear much lighter against the stencil card, but once it has been removed you will see how they resume their tones to contrast strongly with the background. It is a good idea therefore as you work to lift the stencil occasionally to gauge its true effect.

When you are satisfied with the results, leave the paint to dry for a few minutes—then remove the stencil. Lift it off vertically to ensure that any areas still wet do not smudge. Wipe the excess paint off the stencil template and transfer it to the next position.

Holding the can about 15 cm (6 in) away from the stencil, gently press the button using a pumping action to release spray in a series of light bursts. Build up colour gradually in the same way you would with a brush,

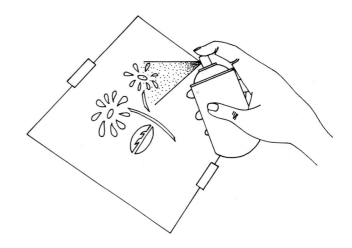

16 *Once you are satisfied that the paint is completely dry, carefully peel back the tape which holds the stencil pattern in place and reveal the stencil. If you are making a continuous frieze, re-position the stencil pattern and repeat the stencilling process.*

Using spray paints

The use of aerosol paints gives finished stencils a soft, misty look and allows two or more colours to be blended together for a subtle, shaded effect. Always follow manufacturers' instructions printed on the back of cans. Work in a well-ventilated room wearing a face mask, protective goggles and rubber gloves to safeguard your skin. Never smoke whilst you work, as aerosols are generally highly inflammable.

Spraying stencils requires a totally different technique to brushwork, so practise first on test stencils until you get the hang of it.

17 *Applying paint using a spray can (top) makes it possible to achieve a smooth graduation of colour (below)*

working from the edges into the middle. Avoid spraying too much paint into one area; this happens if you are holding the can too close to the surface or if the nozzle has become blocked.

Spray paints dry rapidly, so you can check your results almost immediately.

VARIATIONS ON STENCIL TECHNIQUES

Once you have mastered the basics, you may wish to experiment with more advanced stencilling techniques to give the finished image an individual look.

Alternative brush strokes

To give your work a softer quality try altering your brush strokes from the up-and-down pouncing action to smooth circular strokes.

Another alternative, which produces a feathery finish, is to slide the bristles of your brush over the edge of the cut design and back again into the centre of the motif. Lift the brush up, apply a little more paint, then repeat the sliding motion from another side of the design.

Unusual applicators

By using paint pads, natural sponges or small pieces of fabric like velour to dab paint on, you can give stencils an unusual broken colour effect similar to crushed fabric.

Rollers

It is possible to use a roller for stencilling large, simple shapes, particularly where you want an end result of solid colour rather than delicate brush shading. A stencilled floor is the prime example. Rollers waste quite a lot of paint but are much quicker and easier to use than a brush.

The techniques for applying paint with a roller are slightly different than for brushwork. Unlike brushes, rollers never print right into the edges of a stencil, so make sure you cut your designs slightly larger to compensate.

Leave larger margins around the edges of the stencil—at least 7.5 cm (3 in).

Much larger quantities of paint are needed for roller work. Make up a paint store in a bucket and mix smaller quantities to just the right consistency in a mixing bowl. (It should be thin enough to fill in a design shape completely yet dry enough to make the ideal print.)

Pour prepared paint into a roller tray for application and keep a regular check on its consistency when you begin to work. Saturate the roller in paint and roll it on the incline of the tray several times to distribute colour, then remove the excess on scrap paper. Continue this procedure until the roller leaves a solid block of colour with a dry texture.

Practise stencils are vital if you are to become accustomed to the way the roller works.

Roller paint dries slowly, so take great care when removing stencils and clean them thoroughly before repositioning them for further stencilling.

APPLYING TWO OR MORE COLOURS

It is possible to apply different colours through the cut areas of a stencil without using registered overlays.

Simple shapes with broad stencil bridges work best. By using a small brush you can apply colours to a predetermined design. If the stencil has narrow bridges you will need to make a guard to keep the colours separate. This guard can be made from a strip of stencil card or a piece of masking tape that has been pressed repeatedly on to clean fabric to remove some of its stickiness. Use the guard to cover each area of the stencil that you do not want to paint in turn until you have completed the design (fig. 18).

It is possible to employ the same technique for separating colours when you use spray paints.

Stencils have been used to bring interest to the plain peach-coloured walls of this living room. A garland stencil has been repeated in the alcoves, and a spectacular sway provides a focal point above the fireplace.

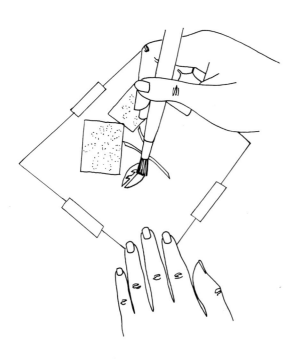

18 *It is possible to use more than one colour on a single stencil by simply masking the areas of the stencil pattern which you want to treat with another colour*

SHADED STENCILS

A common mistake that beginners make is to print or spray paint on too darkly. Colour should be built up gradually from pale to intense. As you become more proficient you will learn how to control the depth of colour, shading a stencil to give it an almost three-dimensional quality. This technique can be particularly effective on items like flowers and fruit.

Using two or more colours through the same stencil opening means you can highlight or shade a motif. Choose light or dark tones of the same colour for a realistic look, and totally different shades for a more original appearance.

First apply an even layer of paint and allow it to dry. Then with the stencil still in place apply the second colour, working along from one edge of the design to the other. As the brush runs out of paint the colour will become lighter and lighter, blending the second colour in with the first. Study real-life shapes and forms to get an idea of how shading works. In general, dark colours applied near the base of the design produce a shaded effect; lighter colours applied nearer the top add highlights.

With a little practice spray paints can be easily controlled to give subtle shading to motifs. Blend two or more different colours to highlight or shade designs. The fine misty quality of spray paint also allows you to overlap colours slightly from one area of the stencil to another for an unusual tonal effect.

REGISTERED OVERLAYS

In Chapter 6 it was explained how to cut stencils with registration marks, for multi-colour motifs or designs that appear to have no stencil bridges. The procedure for using them to reproduce designs is as follows.

Secure the first stencil in place and draw around the notches on either side of it. Print as normal, leave to dry and remove. Tape the second stencil carefully in place, aligning the notch-holes with the pencil marks on the surface underneath and print. Continue with this process until all the component stencils in the design are completed. Erase the pencil marks from the surface. When doing multi-colour stencils, complete everything in one colour first and let it dry fully before applying the next colour; and remember to use a fresh brush for each different colour.

19a *Stem and leaf motif traced onto stencil card and cut out*

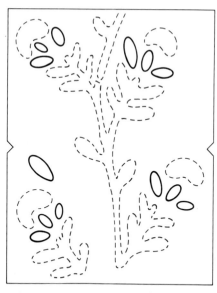

19b *Second-colour stencil of leaves around flower head cut separately*

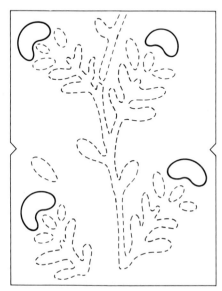

19c *Third-colour stencil for flower heads*

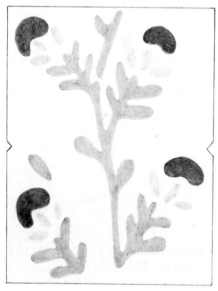

19d *The completed three-colour stencil*

HOW TO POSITION A STENCIL

For small, one-off stencilling projects you may be able to rely on the judgment of your eye for the placement of designs. Larger projects, however, and ones that require repeat stencils across an area must be accurately measured out and marked.

All-over designs

Lengths of fabric and patterned wallpaper are often made up of a single design repeated over and over again in stencilling. First ensure that the stencil design is accurately placed in the centre of the stencil card. Then mark out the surface to be decorated with a grid

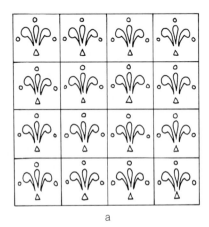

a

b

c

20 *Placing a design in a grid.*
a *When marking up the area you wish to stencil with a grid, each square should be the size of the stencil pattern. This pattern is made by stencilling every square of the grid.*
b *This pattern is made by stencilling alternative squares in the grid.*
c *This pattern is achieved by centring the stencil pattern on the crossing points of the vertical and horizontal lines. Establish the centre point of the stencil pattern by drawing two crossing lines along the halfway point of each side.*

In this Elizabethan room a rich, elegant stencil design has been used to create a complete wall covering effect in place of wallpaper.

corresponding to the size of the stencil. To mark off the surface, first find the centre, then work out from there to the four sides, marking squares or rectangles as you go in pencil or chalk. For accuracy use either a rule and T-square, or a plumb-line.

If your stencil does not correspond to the size of the grid squares, mark the same grid lines on the stencil and use these to align designs when printing. Notches or registration marks on all four sides of the stencil may also help when positioning.

Centering a design
Find the centre of the surface you wish to stencil by drawing diagonal lines from opposite corners and mark with a pencil cross. Make a similar mark in the exact centre of your stencil and align the two when printing.

Borders
First determine how many times the stencil must be repeated to fill the length of surface. Find the centre of the surface to be decorated and then measure the width of the stencil design. Now, starting from the centre of the surface, work out exactly how many design repeats you can fit across it, being careful to include any spacing between repeats in the calculation. If you finish on incomplete designs at either end, try reducing or enlarging the spaces between the motifs. Alternatively you may be able to miss out some parts of the design in the edge repeats or rearrange the shapes in it altogether, adapting to fit the space available.

Corners If a border has to turn a corner there are several alternative ways of dealing with it:

1 Butt the border, by turning the design and placing it at right angles.
2 Mitre the design. First draw a diagonal line at the corner, and then place masking tape on one side of it.

21 *Four different methods of making the corner on a stencil border* **a** *Butting the border.* **b** *A mitred corner on a border.* **c** *Adapting the design slightly to effect a smooth corner curve.* **d** *Using a special corner piece to join the two borders.*

Stencil your border up to the tape and allow it to dry. Remove the tape and place it on the other side of the line. Stencil from the opposite side up to the tape again.
3 Adapt the design by blocking out and filling in certain shapes to produce a gentle curved design that fits round the corner.

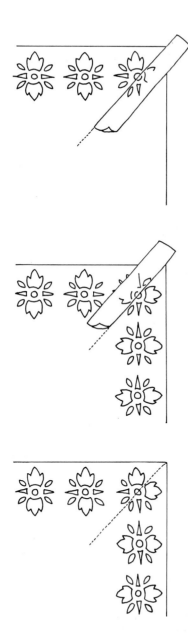

4   Create a special corner design to match the border. Always stencil these first, measuring and spacing the border design in afterwards to meet them.

STENCILLING IN AWKWARD AREAS

A stencil must always lie flat to produce a clean, sharp image. At some point whilst stencilling, however, you may well come across an obstacle in your path like a skirting-board or the mouldings of a window frame that mean your stencil cannot lie flat. There are various solutions to this problem.

If you are working with stencil paper or board you will be able to put a sharp crease in the stencil so that the area you are working on can remain flat, whilst the unused area is resting flush to the obstruction.

Acetate cannot be creased by hand. So if this is your stencil board you will need to score a straight line along

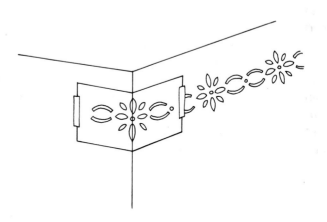

22 Left *Mitring a corner. Draw a diagonal line, place masking tape on one side and stencil the border up to the tape (top). Remove the tape, reposition it along the other side of the line and stencil from the opposite side up to the tape (middle). The completed stencil (below).*
23 Above *Stencilling in an awkward area using a flexible stencil*

53

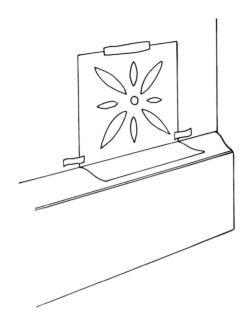

24 *Stencilling in an awkward area—just above the skirting board—using a hinged stencil*

the unused area using a craft knife and steel rule as a guide. Tape over both sides of this score line so that it forms a hinge on the stencil that can be easily bent.

Whilst the two techniques above do not destroy a stencil, they do make it difficult to use again on flat areas. It may therefore be better to cut a separate stencil duplicating just the area of design to be printed. It must be small enough to fit right up to the obstruction.

Where an area is extremely difficult to reach (around pipes, for instance) you will have to paint the stencil design freehand, using a fine fitch brush.

CORRECTING MISTAKES

Small mistakes are rarely noticed on finished stencils, particularly when designs cover a large expanse of wall,

floor or fabric. They may however be more noticeable on fine stencilling detail. The following is a brief guide to the most common errors and how to avoid them.

Smudges on or around the stencil

Apply a coat of clear varnish to stained backgrounds prior to stencilling to make it easier to wipe off mistakes.

Small smudges may be carefully wiped away using a clean rag moistened in the appropriate solvent.

Keep a small pot of the background paint handy for retouching.

To prevent accidental smudging, try to keep your hands as clean as possible whilst you work. Wipe the brushes regularly to prevent them becoming caked and stiff with paint, and check the stencils for excessive build-up of paint which gradually reduces the size of the design and eventually obliterates intricate detailing.

When you have finished stencilling, clean all brushes and stencils thoroughly.

Paint runs

First clean the stencil thoroughly with a damp rag. If the paint run has just made the edges of the design rather fuzzy, try shifting the stencil over very slightly and re-stencilling to sharpen the edges. If the running is more drastic, carefully mask off the other areas of the print and then wipe off the mistake with a cloth moistened with the correct solvent.

If the print is ruined by the paint run, wipe it off as best you can with solvent, repaint the background and start again.

Design faults

Small misjudgments in placement of the design may be corrected in the same way as paint runs. Disastrous misjudgments will have to be wiped off and painted over before re-stencilling.

Two bright stencil designs create a cheerful theme in a child's bedroom. A girl and boy pattern borders the room at picture rail height, and a floral and hearts motif decorates a simple pair of curtains. The patterns have been combined on a chest of drawers.

If the design simply looks rather incomplete, try improvising by filling in gaps with small elements of the original design. Note, however, that this fault should be spotted on test stencils and rectified before you come to positioning designs on the chosen surface.

PROTECTING THE SURFACE

First remove any pencil or chalk registration marks from the surfaces you have decorated with a clean eraser.

In some cases, usually with wall stencilling, this is all you will need to do. Other surfaces that are subject to harder wear benefit from a final coating of varnish. This will preserve the good looks of your stencil and, where powdery paints like poster colour and artists' acrylics have been used, will actually help prolong its life. Leave water-based paints to dry for at least a day before varnishing–two days for oil-based paints.

You can use various matt, satin or gloss finish polyurethane varnishes for stencils applied with a brush or a roller; but only spray varnish should be used on top of spray paints.

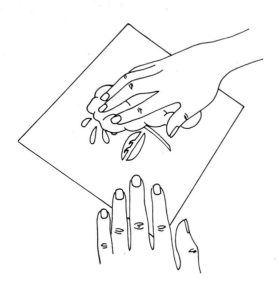

25 *Cleaning the stencil pattern is necessary from time to time during the stencilling process. It prevents excessive build-up of paint which can reduce the size of the design and cause loss of intricate detail.*

8   SURFACES TO STENCIL

In this chapter the procedures and techniques to use for different surfaces are described in greater detail. Suggestions are given on how these surfaces may be decorated and information on the best paints to use for the tasks is also given.

WALLS

Using paint on walls rather than wallpaper gives much greater flexibility with design and colour and allows you to create a totally individual look. Stencils can help you make the most of unusual architectural features or add visual interest to an otherwise plain room.

A border just below the ceiling line provides a simple yet effective touch of decoration; a frieze at dado height can be used to break up large expanses of plain wall. However, don't feel that you must be limited to borders and friezes. When you become more confident about your skills you can attempt all-over designs, panels and so on. If you plan and practise the motifs first on test sheets of paper you can hold these up against the wall to get an idea of their effect.

Preparation of the surface

Walls to be stencilled should be clean, smooth and dry. The more time that is spent getting the walls to this standard the better the end result will be. Start off by taking down curtains, pictures and any easily removable fixtures and fittings that are not to be decorated. Group all

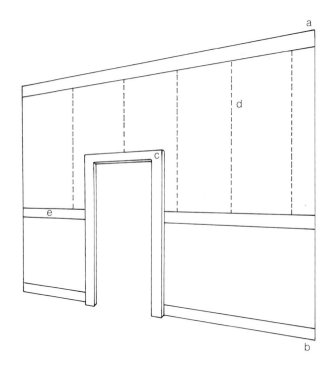

26 *Making use of the architectural features when stencilling a wall.* **a** *ceiling border;* **b** *skirting board border;* **c** *a border round a door;* **d** *overall vertical lines;* **e** *border at dado height.*

the furniture into the middle of the room and cover with dustsheets to protect it.

If the existing paint or wall covering is sound, a thorough clean may be all that is necessary. Brush the walls first, not forgetting picture rails, door and window frames; then wash down everywhere with a grease-cutting proprietary cleaner.

Small areas of damaged wallpaper or peeling paint can generally be smoothed over, but where the surface is in particularly poor condition it may be better to strip it back to the plaster underneath.

Plasterwork

Old plaster may be pitted with small cracks or holes. Fill these with an all-purpose filler, sanding them to a smooth finish once they have dried. If the surface is very shabby, lining paper can be pasted on to provide a smooth, taut surface for paint.

If you are working with new plaster, make sure that it has completely dried out before you begin work, then go over the surface with a scraper to remove any spatters left by the plasterer. Do not sand the surface, as the abrasive glass paper will create scratches. Apply a coat of sealant to prevent any remaining salts in the plaster leaching through and discolouring final layers of paint.

For the most professional finish, apply two coats of undercoat before painting. Thin the first coat down a little to help it bind with the surface underneath and to ensure better adhesion of subsequent coats of paint. Sand in between each layer using very fine sandpaper.

Paints and finishes

In Chapter 4, specific mention was made of the different paints you can use as the base coat for walls. Although there are one or two specialist paints like gesso, in most instances the range of domestic emulsions and eggshells will be perfectly suitable.

Remember, however, to take the different characteristics of the paints into account. Traditional oil-based eggshell, for instance, is smooth and non-absorbent but can be difficult to work with. Silk vinyl emulsion, on the other hand, is more porous in nature but much easier to apply.

A number of different textural effects can be created against the background. The following is a brief guide to some of these special paint effects.

Dragging A specially made oil-based glaze is applied over a base coat of paint; and a wide, long-haired brush is dragged over the surface, removing some paint as it

27 *Dragging*

*A shaded geometric design has been
stencilled onto the corner of a ragged piano.*

goes, to create a series of fine, graduated lines the length of the wall.

Ragging and rag-rolling A room can be ragged simply by dipping a bunch of loosely held rags in paint and pressing them in all directions over a base coat. With rag-rolling, the bundle of rags is rolled rather than dabbed over the surface. Both techniques produce an end result that looks like crushed fabric. Oil-based paints or emulsions can be used for this successfully.

Sponging A very easy technique using a natural sponge dipped in paint to produce a soft, mottled effect. This is an ideal paint finish to use with emulsion.

Stippling Paint is applied with a brush over a base coat, using a dabbing method similar to stencil pouncing, to leave a fine, speckled, mosaic effect. The density of speckles can be varied, depending on the look you want. Both emulsion and oil-based paints can be used.

If you plan to reproduce any of these paint finishes, it is important to read about the techniques in more detail first.

Marking out walls
To help with positioning of designs, measure and mark out various horizontal and vertical lines on the wall.

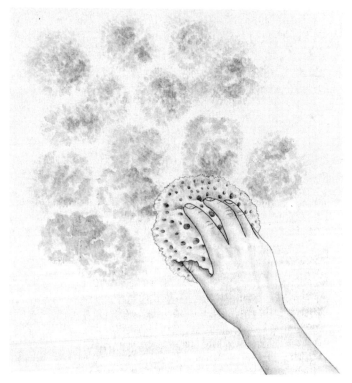

28 *Ragging*

29 *Sponging*

Nine times out of ten you will find that the floors and ceilings in a room are uneven—in old houses they may even slope dramatically. Unless you want to emphasize this unevenness it is best to take all measurements from the line of the skirting-boards and ceilings, so that the stencil designs align visually, rather than being true.

For borders and friezes, mark out horizontal lines using the ceiling and skirting-boards as a guide. Vertical lines to form a grid for all-over designs can then be marked out using a plumb-line and T-square. Use a soft pencil or chalk to mark the paint surface, as they can be rubbed off easily afterwards.

If you need to find the centre of the wall, fix a long piece of string into each top corner and stretch it across to the diagonally opposite corner. The centre is at the point where the two pieces of string cross.

Use all these indicating lines and grids to mark the position of the stencils. Mistakes can be easily rectified at this stage, but not when you are half-way through painting.

If you are using more than one stencilling design in a room, make sure that they are aligned carefully with each other.

Sealing

Traditionally, stencilled walls were left unsealed to allow the paint to develop natural patinas with age, creating a rustic, handmade charm. If you wish to protect your design from undue wear and tear, however, a thin coat of clear matt varnish is easy to apply and allows walls to be wiped clean without damaging the stencil underneath. If you have used spray paints remember to use a compatible spray varnish.

FLOORS

Stencilling is one of the easiest and most effective methods for adding pattern to a floor, and is also a particularly useful way of disguising less-than-perfect wooden boards. Strong visual designs on a floor add weight and balance to a room. Use a simple border to define the shape of the room, or a bold all-over pattern for visual impact. Designs can be made up of delicate floral tracery, imitating oriental carpets, or strong, geometric shapes that copy ceramic tiles.

Preparation of the surface

Floors require much less preparation than walls, but don't skimp on the basics or the results will look messy. Before starting any work, take all of the furniture out of the room; take down any long curtains and remove any fixtures or fittings that are likely to get in the way when you are painting.

Begin by securing loose floorboards and removing any protruding nails or tacks left from the last floor-covering.

Old floorboards will be too dirty to paint and may even have a coat of varnish stain. The quickest and most efficient way of removing this is to hire a floor-sanding machine from a local DIY or hire shop. The shop will tell you how to use the machine. Wood dust has a habit of getting everywhere, so seal the room as best you can and wear a protective mask to prevent inhalation. When you have finished, vacuum up all the dust you can and scrub the floor with water and a little bleach.

Check the floor at this stage for any large cracks or unsightly gouges and fill them. Wood fillers are best, whether you are planning an opaque painted finish or a transparent stain for floorboards. Specially designed for use with woodwork, they expand and contract with the wood and are less likely to shrink and drop out. If you are using a transparent finish, it will be necessary to tint the filler to match other floorboards. Use either water-based paints or the dye or stain you plan to use.

When the filler has dried, you can lightly sand it level. Draughty spaces between floorboards can be filled using thin slivers of wood, planed to fit and hammered and glued in place.

Stains and paints
Various backgrounds can be used for floor stencils.
Bleaching To lighten the wood simply scrub domestic bleach into the surface and then give it a thorough rinse with clean water. Stronger chemical bleaches are available, but these are very caustic and are best left in the hands of an expert.
Staining This adds a colour tint to the floorboards but allows the grain of the wood to show through.

Painting There are no hard-and-fast rules about the number of coats of paint you should apply, or whether the paint is thinned or left in its original consistency. Choose the effect you want to achieve and apply paint accordingly, but bear in mind that water-based paints like emulsion will be more porous than oil-based gloss or glaze. Don't worry about the amount of sheen a paint has; the protective final layer of varnish can be used to provide this.

Measuring and marking out a floor
Border designs are relatively simple to position on a floor. First measure the size of the design and the stencil card itself. Decide how far from the skirting-board you want the design to be and then draw two lines, the depth of the stencil board apart, all the way round the room using chalk and a straight-edged ruler. Position designs so that they look visually correct—this may mean compensating for bowed or out-of-true walls. Mark the position of each individual stencil to see how many repeats fit in along a wall and whether any adjusting is needed (see Chapter 7, page 50).

For an all-over repeated stencil design, you will need to mark out the floor with a grid. Start with a floor plan drawn accurately to scale. This allows you to decide the position of the stencil design on the floor, and also tells you the size the squares will need to be. Mark off the squares along the sides of the plan, working outwards from the centre of each wall. You may need to adjust the size of the squares slightly to ensure that a complete pattern can be fitted in at the edges. If you are using a border with an all-over pattern, mark it in first.

Once you are satisfied with the paper plan you can transfer it to the floor itself. Accuracy is the key to successful floor stencilling. Check all measurements carefully and use only sharp chalk or a pencil and a straight-edged ruler (metal for preference).

A simplified stencil pattern of flowers and leaves has been repeated and reversed to form diamonds in blue and brown across a floor. The design is bordered by a blue stencil pattern.

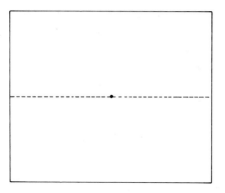

31 *Marking out a floor.*

a *Find the central point of the floor by marking the centre of two opposite walls and joining these points with a line. The mid-point on this line is the central point of the floor.*

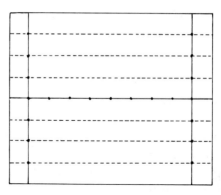

c *Mark square widths along the vertical lines.*

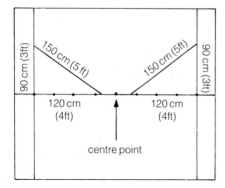

90 cm (3ft) · 150 cm (5 ft) · 150 cm (5ft) · 90 cm (3ft)

120 cm (4ft) · 120 cm (4ft)

centre point

b *Mark off the chosen width of your squares along the centre line. Along the two outer marks draw two lines making sure they are at right angles to the base line.*

d *Complete the grid by joining the dots.*

Even the smallest error in a right angle, for instance, will be magnified when the lines are extended to the other side of a floor. You can use a set square to check right angles, but more accurate on such a large scale is good old Pythagoras' theorem. If two lines are at perfect right angle to one another and you measure 90 cm (3 ft) along one and 120 cm (4 ft) along the other from their crossing point, then a line drawn between each of these measurements should be exactly 150 cm (5 ft). Slightly more than 150 cm (5 ft) indicates that the angle is too wide, slightly less and it is too narrow.

To mark out the floor, first find its central point. Do this by marking the centre of two opposite walls and then use a plumb-line to join up the two parts with a drawn line. The mid-point on this line will be the centre of the room. This line will form the base for all other measurements, and is therefore referred to as the base line.

Starting from the centre point, mark off the chosen width of your squares along both directions of the base line. Through the two outer marks draw two further lines, checking them carefully to ensure they are at right angles to the base line (fig. 31b). Now mark off these two new lines with the chosen width of your squares, again starting from the point where they cross the base line and working out in either direction (fig. 31c).

Draw a line to join the last two marks you have just made on either side of the room parallel to the original base line. Mark accurate square widths across this line and you are now ready to complete the grid by joining up all the dots (fig. 31d).

Once you have constructed the grid you can mark the exact position for each stencil and then begin painting.

Stencilling a floor can be extremely tiring. So take your time and don't feel you have to complete it all in one go.

Sealing
Polyurethane varnish, in a choice of matt, semi-gloss or gloss finishes, is the best way of protecting your newly created floor stencil from normal day-to-day use. For most floors three coats is adequate, but for floors that take a lot of heavy foot traffic, five is better.

First make sure the floor is clean and dry, and check that any pencil or chalk marks have been erased. Use a clean brush to apply the varnish, sanding lightly in between coats for a smooth, professional finish. Often it is a good idea to thin the first coat with the relevant solvent to ensure good adhesion of subsequent coats.

It is advisable to test an unobtrusive area of stencil before applying varnish, to check whether any of the colours bleed. If any tend to run, coat them first with shellac (a traditional barrier paint used on woodwork) before varnishing.

You may need to renew varnish on floors after a year or two, depending on the amount of daily wear it is subject to.

Wax is not generally recommended for stencilled floors; it needs constant renewal to form a protective layer.

Using hardboard on a floor
If after taking up the carpet you discover that the floorboards are in very poor condition or have over-large draughty gaps between them, you can cover them over with hardboard and stencil on top of this. Hardboard cut into manageable sized pieces of about 120 cm (4 ft) square can even be stencilled in sections and fitted together after completion.

For best results, prime the hardboard before painting and choose bold stencil designs.

Divide each piece of hardboard into a squared grid and use this to position designs accurately. Condition the hardboard before laying to prevent it buckling: scrub the backs with water and leave overnight. Tack or glue the pieces into place the following day, being careful to butt the edges closely.

FLOOR-CLOTHS
Floor-cloths, traditional floor coverings and the predecessors of linoleum are made from painted and varnished canvas. Like carpets they can be any size, from a small hearth-side rug to a full room-sized carpet, and can be rolled up and moved from room to room.

When correctly painted and varnished they are extremely durable and will withstand normal foot traffic well. Like linoleum they can be cleaned with a cloth dampened with mild detergent and water.

Making a floor-cloth

The best material to use for a floor-cloth is closely woven canvas, available from sailmakers, specialist canvas shops and artists' suppliers. If widths are too narrow you may need to join several pieces together. Using a hot iron and spray starch, first remove all the creases from the canvas. If you don't do this you will have to pin the canvas out on a wooden frame to stop it getting creased and crinkled as you work. Leave a 2.5 cm to 5 cm (1 in to 2 in) border around the canvas, which will eventually be turned over and stuck down. If you prefer to hem rather than stick the edges, do this now, mitring corners carefully.

Spread newspaper under the canvas and apply two to three coats of oil- or water-based background paint.

Using the techniques described for marking out floors, position the design and stencil. Two to three final coats of polyurethane varnish will protect the floor-cloth against wear.

Finally stick down the raw edges, using a water-soluble craft glue.

FURNITURE

It is often a good idea to pick an item of furniture as the subject for your first stencilling project. It can be prepared and painted in a small work area, and will create a minimum amount of mess. Whilst you should never contemplate stencilling a genuine antique, it is often the solution for bargain finds in the local second-hand shop. Start off with small boxes, trays and shelves before progressing on to larger chairs, tables or chests of drawers.

Be adventurous with your designs, picking out and emphasizing interesting features on the furniture. Tables offer a large expanse for decoration—experiment with simple borders or stencilled place-settings.

Doors can be classed as furniture, too. Treat them rather as a picture, framed by their outer mouldings, choosing either one central design or several smaller ones to fit inside individual panels.

Preparation of the surface

Once again careful preparation pays dividends. If you haven't the time to spare on lengthy preparations, and the piece is not of much importance, you can simply give it a good sanding with fine sandpaper, prior to painting with a base coat.

Shabby and damaged paint or old varnish, however, is better stripped off completely. Various proprietary finish removers are available; use them according to manufacturers' instructions. Check next that the furniture is free of woodworm, glue together any loose joints, and repair any lifting wood veneer. Fill any cracks or holes in the wood with wood filler tinted to match the colour of the wood if you intend just to varnish. Seal any knots in resinous wood with a special knotting paint—this will prevent resin discolouring and cracking the top layers of paint. Finish with a light sanding to level off the surface and provide a key for paint.

Paints and finishes

Pieces to be given a background of paint can then be undercoated and painted. Remember the importance of sanding in between each coat. If you are dealing with new wood, a preliminary coat of primer provides a non-porous base for subsequent layers of paint.

Oil-based gloss paints can be used, but they must be sanded prior to stencilling to give a key for paint to adhere to. Semi-gloss eggshell or porous water-based emulsions are often a better choice. Emulsions can be used effectively to create a naturally aged, chalky appearance and can be sealed with varnish to provide a durable finish. Two coats of paint are usually sufficient, but occasionally a third may be needed.

For a more individual look, choose a specialist paint finish like ragging or dragging (see page 58). Creating a distressed or antiqued background to simulate age and dirt is another specialist technique that can be used to great effect on furniture. There are various ways to achieve this optical illusion, using all kinds of tools and materials including steel wool, sandpaper, rottonstone, wax and burnt sienna glaze. Consult specialist books for greater detail.

Wood stains are an alternative to paint, allowing the natural graining of the wood to show through.

Positioning designs

Follow the instructions given in Chapter 7 for marking out and positioning stencil designs.

Sealing

Use polyurethane varnish to protect the stencil work and bring out the colours in a design.

Three different finishes allow you to choose what degree of sheen to give to your piece. Matt varnish will protect but not shine; satin varnish will give the soft glow of french polish and wax; whilst gloss varnish will provide a hard, shiny effect. Test stencil colours first to ensure they will not bleed—apply shellac if they do.

Make sure the surface to be varnished is clean and dry. Apply the varnish carefully to prevent bubbles forming, and sand in between coats to give a smoother end result. The number of coats of varnish the furniture needs will depend on the type of varnish used and the amount of wear it will be subject to. Matt varnish needs two to three coats, satin four to five, and gloss—for instance, on a table that is to withstand hot plates—may need up to seven coats.

Metallic stencils

By using metallic powders to stencil on to furniture you can create a rich, opulent look. (See Chapter 4, page 24, for more details.)

Prepare the surface with either paints or wood stain and then apply a coat of clear gloss or satin varnish. Leave this until it is almost dry but still tacky. Place the stencil card with your design over the top—it will just stick to the surface. Tip a little metallic powder into a saucer, then dip the end of something like a small foam eye-shadow applicator into the powder. Remove any excess on a paper towel. Now, working outwards from the centre of the design, daub the powder over the cut area of the stencil. Observe the general techniques for stencilling to ensure no powder slips under the cut edge, or you will get a jagged finish. Use clean applicators for different coloured metallic powders.

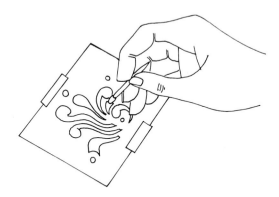

32 *Metallic powders, sometimes known as 'poor man's gold', are available in several finishes ranging from silver to three shades of gold, and they can be used to create a rich, opulent look when stencilling onto furniture, from small jewelry boxes to chair backs. A small foam eye-shadow applicator provides an ideal tool for applying metallic powder to a stencil. Alternatively, use a cotton-wool bud.*

Lift the stencil carefully each time to make sure you don't dislodge any powder. Leave both powder and varnish for twenty-four hours to set, and then wash the surface gently with soapy water to remove excess powder. Finish with a coat of thinned gloss or satin varnish.

An easier way of achieving this exotic look is with metallic spray paints. (See Chapter 7 page 41 for details of application techniques.)

FABRICS

Fabric stencilling gives you the chance to create your own textiles, and opens up a whole new horizon for decorating and design. Start off with simple ideas—a set of place-mats perhaps or a tray cloth. Then when you have got the hang of it you can move on to more ambitious projects.

Adapt patterns from walls or floors in rooms that you have stencilled and print them on lengths of fabric to make up co-ordinating curtains, blinds or chair covers. If this amount of stencilling seems daunting, just print up one or two cushions or a pair of curtain tie-backs; they can work just as well.

Stencilled bed-covers or tablecloths and matching napkins are other alternatives. You can even stencil clothes.

Preparation of the surface

Natural fabrics like cotton and linen are best for stencilling. Their smooth, absorbent surfaces accept dyes readily, and they are available in a variety of weights for different uses. Do take care, though, as absorbency may vary depending on the weave of the cloth; it is always a good idea to test out paint colours first to see if they bleed.

Make sure before you start that the fabric is clean, dry and smooth. Give it a wash to remove any trace of starch or sizing and then iron out the creases. Stretch it out taut over a board or piece of cardboard and secure it with masking tape, dressmakers' pins or drawing-pins.

When you stencil a garment, remember to put several layers of newspaper inside it to prevent colour bleeding through on to the back. If the fabric is to be sewn, make sure that any seams or darts are tacked in place before you start painting, to ensure that the pattern is stencilled as it will appear on the finished article.

Paints

Water-based fabric paints available from craft suppliers are a good choice for this type of stencilling. Once they have been heat-sealed with an iron they become colour fast and can be dry-cleaned or washed on a gentle programme in a machine. Screen printers' dyes and artists' acrylics can also be used. Subtle, shaded looks are easily achieved using conventional stencil brushes.

The more adventurous could try blowing thinned paints through a spray diffuser. Available from artists' suppliers, these give work a speckled, misty finish similar to that of aerosol paints. It is a good idea to weight stencil card down on to the fabric. If you use a diffuser the fine spray of paint has a tendency to drift under the cut edges of a design.

Measuring and marking designs

The basic rules for measuring and marking out designs, as given in Chapter 7, can be applied to fabric stencils. Use an iron to set creases which can be used as guidelines for positioning designs—they can be easily smoothed out afterwards.

Cautionary note

Once you have applied stencil paint, there is no way that it can be removed. Any mistakes you make will have to stay. Beginners should do a test stencil first on a spare piece of fabric and take their time when it comes to the real thing. To avoid accidental smudges, keep your hands scrupulously clean while working.

Sealing

Fabric paints must be heat-sealed so that they adhere to the fibres in the fabric and become waterproof. Pressing with a hot iron is often the quickest and simplest way of doing this, but larger pieces of fabric (curtains or bedspreads, for instance) can be heat-set in a tumble drier on its maximum setting.

It is a good idea to protect fabric from getting dirty too quickly by spraying it with a soil retarder. These will be available from most large department stores and full instructions for their use will be given on the can. If you have used artists' acrylics to paint your designs, always dry-clean, never wash.

OTHER SURFACES TO STENCIL

Leather

Whether you want to restore fading designs on a leather desk top or personalize a favourite plain bag, stencilling is an ideal way of adding both decoration and originality. Bold geometric designs may look best on modern leather items, delicate traceries on traditional pieces, but there are no set rules. Experiment with paper test stencils first until you find a style to suit.

Leather needs little preparation, but should be clean and dry. Leather shoe dyes are the most suitable paints for this kind of stencil work. They are readily available from shoe repairers and department stores, and come in a wide range of colours. Acrylics and cellulose-based aerosol paints can also be used.

Follow the basic instructions given in Chapter 7 for measuring and marking your stencil design.

Once the stencil is completed, it may not always be necessary to seal the surface if a leather dye was used as they contain their own protective finish. If you prefer to use a sealant, however, a coat of polyurethane varnish can be applied directly on to the paint once it has completely dried, but do not varnish unpainted areas of leather. Wax furniture polish may also help seal paint colours on to leather, but test a small area first to guard against the paint bleeding or changing colour dramatically.

Ceramics

Stencils can be applied to both porous and non-porous ceramic surfaces. Use them to liven up plain glazed tiles and clay flowerpots.

Check that surfaces are clean, dry and free from grease and dust.

Choose between cellulose spray paints, acrylic colours and Japan paints. It is also possible to use oil-based eggshell over a base covered with a specialist oil-based glaze.

Follow the basic instructions given in Chapter 7 for measuring and marking out a design.

Stencilled designs on porous ceramics may be left unsealed to age naturally and take on a rustic look. To seal designs, apply a coat of matt or glass polyurethane varnish once the paint has dried.

Metal

Yet another surface that can be decorated with stencilled designs is metal. You may want to co-ordinate a dull metal filing cabinet with other decor in the room, or to break up the expanse of plain white metal on a fridge, dishwasher or freezer. Even the smallest cake tins and old metal trays can be transformed with the use of stencils.

First treat any rust spots on old metal with rust removers and then clean the surface down with soapy water and dry thoroughly. For both old and new metal you should then rub the surface down with fine wire wool and apply a coat of metal primer or red oxide. Sand lightly to give a key for subsequent coats of paint.

Finally apply one or two coats of oil-based paint. Cellulose spray paints are the best as they are designed specifically for use on metal. Acrylic paints can also be used but must be thoroughly sealed.

Follow the basic instructions in Chapter 7 for measuring and marking out your design, and stencil.

Spray paints can be protected with spray varnish; acrylics and Japan paints with polyurethane varnish.

STENCIL PATTERNS

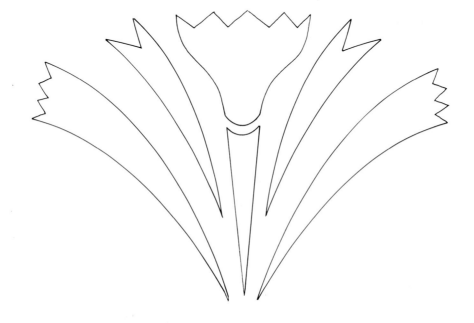

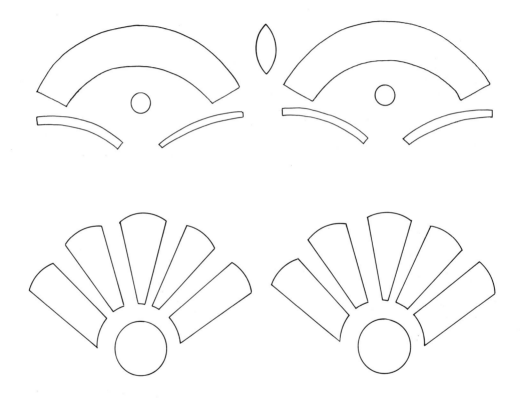

INDEX

Page numbers in *italics* refer to illustrations